TRAVELLING LIGHT

Daily Bible meditations for student electives

All Bible quotes are from the
New International Version (NIV)
unless otherwise stated.

Emphases and capitalisation
added by authors and editor.

Readings from Week 4 day 25 and
Week 8 day 50 are adapted by kind
permission of Dr James Burton OBE

Readings from Week 4 day 28 and
Week 8 days 52-55 used with kind
permission of The International
Christian Medical & Dental Association.

For more information
about CMF's international ministries,
visit our website at www.cmf.org.uk

Contents

Contents

Introduction

Your word is a lamp to my feet
And a light for my path
Psalm 119:105

You are about to set off on an exciting journey - a journey of discovery. A developing world elective is a fantastic opportunity to learn about health and disease in a different context, to live within another culture, and to begin to understand life's realities for the majority of the world's population. Enriching but challenging, it may put your faith to the test. You may find yourself questioning some assumptions and reconsidering what is important.

This book is a companion for your journey, designed to help you shine the light of God's word on your experiences and look at people and places through God's eyes. It contains readings and reflections from health professionals who have lived and worked in the developing world, offering encouragement, insight and fresh challenges.

Reading the Bible every day will radically affect your Christian life. If you have never done this or have let other things get in the way, an elective is a great opportunity to get into the habit of spending time with God every day. The readings cover a two-month cycle. You may want to begin before you go – just as you start your malaria prophylaxis! Pray that God will speak to you through his word, and give yourself time to meditate and pray about what you have read. Use these times to lay before him your hopes, fears, doubts and questions and to pray for the situations and people around you.

My prayer for you as you set off is that your elective will broaden your horizons and deepen your relationship with God – for most it will be a life-changing experience. I also pray this book will be a light for you to travel by, every step of the journey.

Vicky

Vicky Lavy
Head of International Ministries
Christian Medical Fellowship

Contributors

Peter Armon	worked for many years in Tanzania and Malawi as an obstetrician and gynaecologist before becoming CMF's Overseas Support Secretary until 2008
Peggy Burton	worked for several years as a missionary nurse in the Democratic Republic of Congo
Kate Cheesman	did a medical elective in Belo Horizonte, Brazil
Liz Croton	went to the Caribbean for a medical elective
Douglas Fishlock	worked as a physician in the Middle East and in the Arctic
Mark Forshaw	originally trained as a health service manager, and has worked with Africa Inland Mission in Kenya, with World Health Organisation and ACET-UK, a Christian HIV and AIDS support organisation
Sally-Ann Jenkins	was the student worker for Christian Student Nurses and Midwives Fellowship for several years and is a founder of Christian Nurses and Midwives
Steven Fouch	is a nurse by training and is currently the Head of Allied Professions at CMF. He has worked on short-term missions in North Africa and cross-cultural church planting in South London
Marjory Foyle	served as a medical missionary in South Asia before training in psychiatry and returning to India. Author of the book 'Honourably Wounded', she has specialised for over a decade in supporting traumatised mission personnel
Janet Goodall	is a retired paediatrician based in the UK
Claire Hollingsworth	writes from her experience of working in the prisons of Zambia on a Medics Tearfund Transform Team

Mary Hopper	worked for many years as a missionary nurse in Zimbabwe and now lectures at Oxford Brookes University
Ernst A Jacobsen	is a physician based in Denmark
Sophia Lamb	spent time in China as a medical student and is now a missionary in Hong Kong
Helen Malcolm	is a physician based in Australia
Mark Marno	did a nursing elective in West Africa and later worked as a UCCF link worker for nursing students
Douglas Noble	did a medical elective in Africa and later worked in China with the Jian Hua Foundation
Gareth Payne	did an elective in Botswana as a medical student
Ian Spillman	worked for several years as the Medical Superintendent at Kisiizi Christian Hospital in Uganda, and is now a paediatrician based in UK
Alan Vogt	is the prayer co-ordinator for the Christian Dental Fellowship, and an active supporter of dentists in mission
Jenny Wordley	did a dental elective in Mexico and later became the director of Dentaid, a charity that provides refurbished dental surgeries for developing countries

Praise be to the God and Father
of our Lord Jesus Christ!
In his great mercy he has given us
new birth into a living hope through
the resurrection of Jesus Christ
from the dead, and into an inheritance
that can never perish, spoil or fade
— kept in heaven for you!

1 Peter 1:3&4

Week 1

Hope

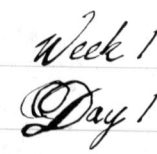

A 'prisoner of hope'

Peter Armon begins a series about hope in hopeless situations

BIBLE REF:
Zechariah 9: 9 - 13

BIBLE VERSE:
Return to your fortress, O prisoners of hope.

It's amazing how often you can read the Bible and still come across words and phrases that trigger off new ideas and patterns of thought. In this passage, God is calling his people to rejoice over the fact that their King is coming. He is not yet here, but certainly on the way. A righteous King who will speak peace to the nations (Isaiah 9: 5).

He is referring to an event and a Person with whom we are now very familiar from where we stand in time. He is talking about Jesus. He reminds us that one day Jesus will rule the whole earth (Psalm 72: 8 - 11 and Philippians 2: 10 - 11). As he goes on talking to them, God refers to his hearers as '*prisoners of hope*' (v12).

From the world's point of view the situation the Jews faced at that time was pretty hopeless. They were an impoverished people recently returned from a long exile in captivity and yet God calls them '*prisoners of hope*'. Hopeless and helpless from the world's point of view but '*prisoners of hope*' from God's perspective. They are bound to a sure and certain promise that God has given them. It will come to pass.

Do you remember what Jeremiah had said some years previously? (Jeremiah 29: 11). He had quoted God as saying '*I know the plans I have for you ... plans to prosper you and not to harm you, plans to give you HOPE and a future*'.

One could also say the disciples faced a pretty hopeless situation immediately after the crucifixion. All their hopes of being part of a victorious kingdom had been dashed. But Jesus' resurrection appearances changed all that. He brought hope to the hopeless and turned their world upside down and right side up.

The biblical meaning of the word 'hope' is 'a confident and eager expectation of something good'. No wonder that Paul prays so earnestly for the Ephesian church that the *'eyes of [their] heart might be enlightened in order that [they] may know the HOPE to which he has called [them]'* (Ephesians 1: 18).

Are things around or within you looking pretty hopeless at present? James calls us to *'consider it pure joy'* when we face various trials (James 1: 2) and goes on to explain why. Peter calls us to take up a position of praise because even in such situations we need to remember that God, *'in his great mercy ... has given us new birth into a living HOPE'* (1 Peter 1: 3, but please see vs3 - 9).

> They were an impoverished people recently returned from exile and yet God calls them 'prisoners of hope'.

PRAYER & ACTION
Put Paul's prayers to the Ephesians recorded in chapters 1: 17 - 19 and 3: 16 - 19 into the first person, and pray them today and every day.

Biblical hope

Peter Armon explains what hope in God really means

BIBLE REF:
Romans 5: 1 - 11

BIBLE VERSE:
And we rejoice in the hope of the glory of God.

As I said yesterday, biblical hope can be defined as 'a confident and eager expectation of something good'. This isn't the 'if' or 'maybe' of the world's view of hope. There isn't uncertainty about it. Biblical hope is based on the sure and certain promises of a God who is faithful to his word. Both Solomon at the beginning of his reign and Joshua at the end of his life could testify to the faithfulness of God both in their lives and the lives of others around them (see I Kings 8: 56 and Joshua 23: 14 - 15).

There are three basic ingredients to this hope - confidence, expectancy and security. It's not a matter of believing that everything will always go well, that we will never have any problems as a Christian and that life will be a bed of roses for us. It is knowing that God is in control; that he loves us and will always be there for us.

It was the faith and confident expectation shown by three young men as they faced a furious and powerful king and a blazing fiery furnace who could say '*the God we serve is able to save us ... But even if he does not ... we will not serve your gods*' (Daniel 3: 17 - 18). It was the sort of hope that sustained Jesus as he prayed to his Father that he might be spared the cross of Calvary, which enabled him to say '*not as I will but as You will*' (Matthew 26: 39, 42, 44).

Such hope creates within the person who has it an inner attitude of openness towards God, other people and to life. This is important because we only experience what we receive and we will only receive what we are open to.

Such hope is the foundation of our faith (Hebrews 11: 1). It makes us bold to witness (2 Corinthians 3: 12). It is an anchor for the soul (Hebrews 6: 19) and it is a helmet of salvation (1 Thessalonians 5: 8) protecting our minds when doubt, fear and anxiety come. Such hope comes from knowing God. And so Paul writes:

May the God of hope fill you with all joy and peace as you trust in him, so that you may overflow with hope by the power of the Holy Spirit (Romans 15: 13)

> Biblical hope is based on the sure and certain promises of a God who is faithful to his word.

PRAYER & ACTION
Make the words of Romans 15: 13 written above into a personal prayer today, remembering that our God is a faithful God (1 Corinthians 1: 9).

Look up the other verses about hope quoted above and prayerfully meditate upon them.

The little foxes

A warning about destructive thoughts that can destroy our hope

BIBLE REF:
Song of Solomon
2: 1 - 17

BIBLE VERSE:
Catch for us ...
the little foxes
that ruin the
vineyards.

I n this beautiful love song, we read in allegorical terms of the delights and security of a love relationship with Jesus. Of a Lover who tells us that winter is past and a *'season of singing has come'* (v12); who calls us to come away with him (v10); of a beloved who can confidently sing, *'I am my Beloved's and he is mine. And his banner over me is love'* (v4).

But in the midst of it all is a warning about little foxes. Little foxes that can do a great deal of harm; that can 'ruin the vineyards' if they are not dealt with; that will grow into bigger foxes that could conceivably do even greater harm. I don't intend us to get into a discussion about the ethics of fox hunting but the writer is telling us something important here!

The writer warns us that little foxes need to be dealt with **quickly** - while the vines are still in bloom, **radically** - **all** of them need to be caught and that *not* **dealing with them** could ruin the fruit we hope to produce.

Ask yourself, in the context of our thinking about hope, what these little foxes might represent to you personally.

Perhaps it is that we are allowing ourselves to harbour thoughts that question or deny the faithfulness of God? There will certainly be many occasions as you come up against the seemingly insurmountable problems facing the poor of this world when you will cry out 'God, why?' and feel 'It's so unfair', 'How can a loving God allow this to happen?' Questions to which we often have to admit there are no easy answers. But questions to which you might feel there is an answer 'if only...' But you also know the answer might be costly for you and too costly for a self-seeking and greedy world to face.

If we allow these thoughts to deceive us into thinking that God doesn't care and there is no hope, then we are allowing these little foxes to do their work. Thoughts that are not dealt with can lead to careless words spoken out against God or others, and they may lead to actions (or inaction) that we will later regret. Paul tells us that he takes 'captive every thought to ... Christ' (2 Corinthians 10: 5). Surely an example we should follow.

Whatever it means for you - seek out those little foxes. Be ruthless with them. Destroy them before they destroy you, your relationship with your heavenly Father and the fruit that the Holy Spirit is growing in your life.

There will be many occasions as you come up against the problems facing the poor of this world when you will cry out 'God, why? It's so unfair'.

PRAYER & ACTION

Find time today to meditate upon this love song and then to sit quietly with God and ask him to search your heart. Be honest with yourself. Are there things you need to deal with if your faith and hope are to stay strong and grow? Remember there is nothing you have done or can do that will cause him to love you any less, just as there is nothing you can do that will cause him to love you any more. Confess any sins you need to deal with and know that 'he is faithful and just and will forgive us our sins and purify us from all unrighteousness' (1 John 1: 9).

A prescription for anxiety: a nun's story

Peter describes a Christian's response to anxiety

BIBLE REF:
Philippians 4: 4 - 9

BIBLE VERSE:
...the peace of God which transcends all understanding will guard your heart and your mind in Christ Jesus.

She hadn't looked particularly happy when she walked through the door. In fact she looked distinctly anxious and depressed.

It's not every day that a bevy of nuns walks into the Gynae clinic and this group included their Mother Superior! They sat down together while the 'patient' described her symptoms and she then retired to the adjacent examination room where I examined her. There were no signs of any physical disease and it seemed to me more a problem of an emotional or spiritual 'dis-ease', which was producing physical symptoms. We had a long chat together and then I wrote out a prescription and handed it to her and they left the clinic.

A few minutes later, there was a commotion outside the door and they burst back in.
'We've just read what you have written on the prescription pad. Can you teach us to sing it?'
I had in fact written out the words of an old chorus I had learnt as a child.

■ *All your anxieties, all your cares*
■ *Take to the mercy seat, leave them there*
■ *Never a burden he cannot bear*
■ *Never a friend like Jesus.*

The next 10 minutes were taken up by an impromptu 'choir' practice in the clinic while I taught them the tune, then off they went. I could hear them singing their way down the corridor and off into the distance.

PRAYER & ACTION

Yesterday we were thinking about the little foxes that can destroy our fruitfulness. Perhaps anxiety is another one that needs to be dealt with. The passage we have read today gives us Paul's prescription for anxiety and he has written four items on his pad. They are best taken and applied as prescribed, and you can be reassured that there is no risk from an overdose. Make them the basis of your prayers and actions today:

- Rejoice and give thanks always and in every situation - verses 4 and 6.
- Pray in every situation and about everything - verse 6.
- Think and fill your minds with the things listed - verse 8.
- Put what you read in God's word into practice - verse 9.

The prognosis is good - for you will experience that *'the peace of God which transcends all understanding, will guard your hearts and your minds in Christ Jesus'* (v7) and that *'the God of peace will be with you'* (v9). What it is to be in the safe hands of the greatest Physician of them all!

What it is to be in the safe hands of the greatest Physician of them all!

God is good

Peter Armon explains how Paul found the secret of contentment in difficult circumstances

BIBLE REF:
Philippians 4: 10 - 20

BIBLE VERSE:
My God will meet all your needs according to his glorious riches in Christ Jesus.

They say that '*hope springs eternal in the human heart*', but there comes a time when recurring disappointment can lead to despair. 'If God is good then why did this or that happen (or not happen)?' 'Why did he let me down?'

We've looked at the need to nip such thoughts in the bud and not allow them to take hold of our minds where they will fester and affect our emotions. Writing in his book 'Christ Empowered Living', Selwyn Hughes points out that the line the devil took in tempting Adam and Eve in the Garden of Eden was '*to insinuate a doubt into Eve's **mind** concerning the goodness of God. Once that doubt is entertained it soon affects the way she felt about God in her **emotions**. Then doubting God and disliking God (because of his limitation on her freedom) the next step is **disobedience**.*' That disobedience led to **rebellion** (sin) and its consequence was separation from God.

In the verses we have read today, Paul reminds us that God is good and that God's goodness is often demonstrated through the actions of friends who love us and express that love through caring practically for our needs. Paul knew what it was to be in need, but he had learnt an important and invaluable lesson that we all need to learn and relearn - '*the secret of being content in every situation*' (v12). He had also learnt that he could do this and '*everything through [Christ] who gives me strength*' (v13).

Just as we need to learn to distinguish between needs and wants, so we need to discern the difference between attempting to do '*all things*' (which can lead to burnout) and doing the things that Christ has asked us to do (which leads to fulfilment). When we are living in the knowledge that God is good, that he does supply all our needs and that we can do all the things that he asks us to, we like Paul can '*rejoice greatly in the Lord*' (v10).

> God's goodness is often demonstrated through the actions of friends who love us.

PRAYER & ACTION

- Read and meditate on Psalm 103.
- Look back over your life and rejoice in the ways in which you have experienced the goodness of God and give him thanks.
- Ask God to show you what are the things he wants you to be doing today and set about doing them. Remember, he demands obedience, not necessarily success, in all that you attempt for him.
- Write a letter or email a friend and thank them for being a practical demonstration of the goodness of God to you.

You'll never walk alone

Today's reading looks at God's faithfulness in all situations

BIBLE REF:
Hebrews 13: 5 - 6

BIBLE VERSE:
I will never leave you or forsake you.

The Amplified version of the Bible puts Hebrews 13:5 like this: *'God himself has said, I will not in any way fail you nor give you up nor leave you without support. I will not, I will not, I will not in any degree leave you helpless nor forsake you nor let you down or relax My hold on you! Assuredly not!'*

My wife and I went off to Spain to work with a missionary group in 1990. We had worked overseas before in Africa - each time in paid government employment but in a missionary context. On one of the occasions we knew that we wouldn't have enough to live on as a family when we set out, but we trusted that God would supply our needs, and he did. Really, we were going 'without any visible means of support'. We were living 'by faith', which I think by the way is a silly term, as Galatians 2: 20 makes it plain that we all live by faith - not ours but God's, and what matters more is that God is **always** faithful to us.

As we set off for Spain it was really quite scary. As we prayed about it, God gave us the verse quoted above (v5), and told us to put our names into it. Three times in this verse, God personally told us that he could be trusted not to let us down. It's easy to look back through the 'retrospectoscope' and say 'hallelujah! he did it!' But at the time, we went sustained only by that sure and certain hope that he would keep his word, and he did. It's a lesson we have had to learn and relearn on many occasions during our lives.

When Jesus sent his disciples out into all the world, he promised that he would go with them and stay with them - even to the end of the age (Matthew 28: 20). Paul reminds us that nothing in all the world can separate us from the love of God (Romans 8: 38 - 39). Hang on to these words today if you are feeling lonely. I can truly testify to the fact that God never changes (verse 8 of the text). He is true to his word and he will be true to you as you seek to serve him.

In the rest of the chapter, the writer exhorts us to get on with living the Christian life: loving one another, being hospitable, remembering those in need and doing something about it, keeping our lives free of immorality and the love of money, sticking to the truth of God's word, and doing good to one another. We are also called to honour, imitate and obey our leaders **and** to pray for them, and to do all this with a spirit of praise on our lips (verse 15). That's a tall order you might say!

If it all seems too difficult, if not impossible, then the writer prays a beautiful prayer for us in the midst of which he reminds us that God has equipped us *with everything good for doing his will* (vs20, 21).

> We went sustained only by that sure and certain hope that he would keep his word, and he did.

PRAYER & ACTION
Read again the prayer of Paul in Ephesians 3: 14 - 21 and make it your own. If you are feeling down and wondering how you will make it through the day, realise that you're not alone. Read again about Moses' tussle with God in Exodus 3 and 4, and about Gideon in Judges 6 and Elijah in I Kings 19, and take heart. Even heroes of the faith have tough times, and Jesus understands (Hebrews 4: 14 - 16). Think and pray out of these verses.

Give thanks in all circumstances

Peter Armon looks at Habakkuk, a man of faith in devastating times

BIBLE REF:
Habakkuk 3: 1 - 19

BIBLE VERSE:
Though everything about me is falling apart and I have nothing to live on 'Yet will I rejoice in the Lord'.
(v17, 18 paraphrased)

I wonder how easily you found your way to this book in the Bible? Habakkuk is one of those little books at the end of the Old Testament that you miss if you blink as you're flicking through the pages. We don't know much about him, even how to pronounce his name, but he's one of those characters that I'm looking forward to meeting in heaven and finding out more about. Probably the most memorable words he wrote are found in Habakkuk 2: 4, *'the righteous will live by his faith'*.

Our chapter is headed in the NIV 'Habakkuk's Prayer'. And what an interesting prayer. I don't know how you pray but here is a man who *'stands in awe'* of God's deeds and yet a man who is not afraid to enter into a conversation with him; arguing and asking questions, trying to find out how God felt, pleading with him in effect to, *'do it again in my day God'* (v2). Almost saying, 'I'm fed up with reading about what You did long ago - do it today, Lord'.

Notice as the prayer progresses how the pronouns change from the impersonal 'he' (vs3 - 7) to the more personal 'you' (vs8 - 15) and even back to 'I' (vs16 - 19). Are you on such personal terms with God? It seems that as Habbakuk takes the time to meditate on God's deeds, so he comes deeper into his presence and feels safe to open up his heart - though *'[it] pounded and my lips quivered'* as he did so (v16). His meditation leads him to the same place as that of Daniel's three friends (Daniel 3: 17 - 18). Whatever may happen to him - and verse 17 describes a pretty awful state of crop failure and death of his animals, leading presumably to hunger and possibly starvation - he is prepared to say '*yet I will rejoice in the LORD*'.

It's perhaps too easy for us in the West to quote Paul's words to the Philippians - '*Rejoice in the Lord always*' (Philippians 4:4). But here is a man who was able to do that. It may be that you are facing a situation today where those around you are living in poverty and facing hunger and starvation. What do you say to them? What can you say?

We can but walk in obedience to God's word and be thankful for his goodness to us while reaching out to those in need and sharing our wealth with them in whatever way we can, in however insignificant a way that may seem. God will bless you as you do so today.

Here is a man who stands in awe of God's deeds and yet is not afraid of asking questions.

PRAYER & ACTION

- Try and turn Habbakuk's prayer into a song and let his words minister to your heart.
- Ask God to show you how you can appropriately share the comparative wealth he has given you with the needy folk you will meet today. Remembering that '*whatever you did for one of the least of these brothers of mine you did for me*' (Matthew 25: 40).
- Read I Peter 1: 3 - 9. Be honest with yourself (and God) but seek to praise him and greatly rejoice in the hope he has given us, and determine to develop a lifestyle of thankfulness where you are giving thanks in all circumstances.

If we are thrown into the blazing furnace, the God we serve is able to save us from it, and he will rescue us from your hand, O king. But even if he does not, we want you to know, O king, that we will not serve your gods or worship the image of gold you have set up.

Daniel 3:17 & 18

Daniel:
living for God across
the cultural divide

Feeling alone in a foreign community

Douglas Noble begins a series on Daniel and his stand for God in a foreign land

BIBLE REF:
Daniel 1: 8 - 17

BIBLE VERSE:
God gave knowledge and understanding of all kinds of literature and learning.

I don't know what has inspired you to travel so far for your elective placement. But one thing I do know is that the environment you now find yourself in is very different to home. Perhaps you are wondering how you will cope.

In this passage we find Daniel and his three friends in a very similar situation to you. The king of Babylon has taken them to his palace for a very privileged education. However, the environment they found themselves in was completely foreign to them. They were surrounded by people who did not know the God of the Hebrews. Their fellow students had a very different lifestyle, enjoying all that the king had to offer. In spite of the pressure from this foreign community with its decadent way of life, Daniel and his three friends chose to be different (v8). They decided to make a stand and show those around them a different and better way. Ultimately this brought them great reward (vs15, 17).

Working in a hospital far from home can be very daunting. Like Daniel and his friends, you will find yourself surrounded by many people who know nothing of your faith or way of life. Some of them may mock you or be critical of your way of life. They may not appreciate why you live your life the way you do. They may, like the chief of the eunuchs (v10), wrongly suppose that your way of life is restrictive and damaging. At such times, like Daniel and his friends, you need to rest assured in the promises you have from God. If you believe in his ways and obey his commands, he will be with you no matter how difficult the task ahead may appear. Although you won't always be rewarded like Daniel (v17), you can find assurance in the knowledge of your salvation through Christ and the great reward that awaits you when this life is over.

Daniel and his three friends chose to be different.

PRAYER & ACTION
Spend some time asking God for wisdom, strength and the determination to live distinctively as a Christian.

Ask him to help you put his word into practice each day.

Week 2
Day 9

Dealing with irrationality

Douglas Noble looks at the importance of prayer

BIBLE REF:
Daniel 2: 13 - 19

BIBLE VERSE:
Then Daniel explained the matter to his friends. He urged them to plead for mercy from the God of heaven concerning this mystery, so that he and his friends might not be executed.

I read recently in a newspaper of an English tourist who was raped and shot in South Africa. It all seemed so meaningless and pointless. Why was her dignity of so little consequence to her attackers? Surely she did not deserve this.

You may see some pretty unpleasant things on your medical elective. You may come across families and communities who are treated unjustly by local authorities. You may encounter children who suffer because of the ruthless actions of others.

Daniel and his three friends found themselves in a similar situation. Things seemed to have been going well for them. They had managed to maintain their distinctive lifestyle in a foreign environment and had not compromised their beliefs. But now they are faced with the irrational actions of Nebuchadnezzar the king (v13). The question is: how will they cope? Daniel is quite clear how he and his friends must proceed. They must pray (v18).

Prayer has two major functions in Christian life. It purifies the mind, enabling us to understand more clearly the ways of God, and it allows us to ask God for answers to our difficulties. That is exactly what Daniel and his friends did in response to the irrational actions of Nebuchadnezzar. And God gives them the answer (v19).

PRAYER & ACTION

- Wherever you find yourself today, stop, pray and ask God to guide you. Ask him too, to increase your understanding of matters that seem unresolvable. He may not tell you, as he did for Daniel, the meaning of the dreams of others, but he will guide you and protect you as you tend to the needs of others.

- Thank God that no situation takes him by surprise. Resolve to make prayer a first resort when you find yourself in difficult situations.

Daniel is quite clear about how he and his friends must proceed. They must pray.

Embracing the miraculous

God can use us even in situations we can't understand

Do miracles still happen today? This question is a regular challenge to Christians. We have all heard stories of healings and miracles, and it is ironic that these things always seem to happen so far from home! Perhaps you will see a miracle while on your medical elective. Or perhaps you will come across something that you cannot explain - a real mystery.

This was the situation Daniel found himself in when he revealed to Nebuchadnezzar the king the meaning of his dream. It was such a strange dream and it may refer to the empires that were to follow Nebuchadnezzar's reign. In all honesty, no one is quite sure what it all means. What is certain is that God wished to communicate to this king that he was not all-powerful and that his kingdom would not last forever. In fact, he was telling him that it would be destroyed (vs39, 44). God tells Nebuchadnezzar that only his Kingdom will last forever and in so doing revealed a great mystery to him.

I'm sure you have already encountered many things on your trip that seem mysterious. I would urge you to take heart from the interpretation of this dream. When Daniel was under the threat of death, God revealed the unknowable to him, so that he could show an unscrupulous king that only God was immortal.

Perhaps God will show you something similar today. His Spirit may direct you to a person who desperately needs to hear that forgiveness and acceptance by God are possible. You may have the privilege of explaining the greatest mystery of all, the mystery of the cross - that Christ has died once for all who believe and obey him (Ephesians 1: 9 - 10).

When Daniel was under the threat of death, God revealed the unknowable to him.

PRAYER & ACTION

- Spend some time thanking God that he is able to do more than all we expect or imagine (see Ephesians 3: 20).
- Ask him to give you the opportunity to share the Gospel with someone today.

Surviving suffering: standing firm

Douglas describes a crisis that led him to reflect on suffering

BIBLE REF:
Daniel 3: 12 - 18

BIBLE VERSE:
... the God we serve is able to save us from it, and he will rescue us.

I was working in Africa at the start of 2002 in a mission hospital near Durban. I will never forget the day I was pricked with a needle while doing a femoral artery stab on a lady with suspected diabetic ketoacidosis. I knew that almost 50% of the patients in the hospital were HIV positive. I clearly remember going back to the small, hot and dusty room in the hospital where I was staying and crying my heart out.

Over the next few days I thought deeply about the suffering that faces Christians all over the world and the insecurity that suffering brings. I began to understand what it is like not knowing what is going to happen next in your life or how everything may suddenly change for the worse. I thought about Christ and the cross and how much he and the apostles suffered for their faith (Philippians 3: 10).

In this chapter, Daniel's three friends face great suffering. Imagine what it must have been like for them when they refused to bow down before this pagan idol (v12), and the suffering they and their friends and family must have gone through when the order was given for them to be thrown into the fiery furnace (v20).

We can learn so much from their attitude to this terrible suffering (vs17 - 18). They were prepared to die for their faith and accepted that God might not deliver them, but allow them to suffer in order that his greater purposes be realised. Whatever was going to happen, they were absolutely resolute in their commitment to follow God's way for them and not compromise their faith by bowing down to the image of gold. Perhaps today you will be called to face some suffering for your faith. Thankfully God protected Daniel's friends. And in my case, although not anything like on the same scale, the patient I treated was HIV negative and my anxiety came to an end. The question is, will you be prepared to suffer like these three men when there is no guarantee of deliverance?

> They were prepared to die for their faith and accepted that God might not deliver them.

PRAYER & ACTION
Thank God that he is able to save you from any fiery trial you may face today.

Spend some time praying for yourself, and for others working with you, for the strength to stand firm in the face of trials.

Surviving suffering: showing God's power

God uses suffering to teach and refine us

BIBLE REF:
Daniel 3: 19 - 29

BIBLE VERSE:
Look! I see four men walking around in the fire, unbound and unharmed, and the fourth looks like a son of the gods.

We have all heard wonderful stories of Christians who were persecuted and stood firm in their faith. But why does God allow us to suffer at all? Surely if he truly loved us we would not have to suffer.

The Bible teaches something quite different. Since the whole of the Christian message is based on suffering and, in particular, the suffering of the Son of God on the cross for our sins, it is astonishing that we should expect our Christian lives to be free from suffering.

The Bible teaches us that it is good for us to endure suffering for a while, so that we might be more like Christ who endured the ultimate suffering for us (Romans 5: 3; James 1: 2). We also know that Jesus is with us during these times.

Imagine what it was actually like for Daniel's friends in the furnace (v23). The Lord appears to them, unties them and assures them their ordeal will not last much longer. He tells them that he has to show the king that he rescues his people, and even though they are humiliated, he remains with them so that they will learn perseverance.

One of my lasting memories from my limited medical work on the mission field in both Africa and China is the courage and perseverance of older and wiser Christians. I remember long nights when I would quiz the missionaries at length about their experiences and was constantly amazed at how much they had come through over the years.

Hudson Taylor, who was perhaps the most famous missionary to China, is a great example of a man who was prepared to go to any length to show Christ's love and make him known. Despite losing his young wife and experiencing endless suffering, he never gave up. People like that show us how God has used the most turbulent experiences to prepare his servants for the task of leadership.

It is astonishing that we should expect our Christian lives to be free from suffering.

PRAYER & ACTION

- Look back at key events in your Christian life. Think about situations that seemed hard at first but where in hindsight you can see God lovingly at work.
- Give thanks for those times and commit to him any current difficulties, asking for help to persevere and press on.

God humbles the proud

God will bring justice in his time

BIBLE REF:
Daniel 4: 24 - 34

BIBLE VERSE:
Therefore,
O king,
be pleased
to accept
my advice:
Renounce your
sins by doing
what is right.

I remember on one occasion travelling across Western China to a little village on the Tibetan plateau and being astonished at the level of poverty. However, in the midst of the poverty was also great wealth, enjoyed by a select few. Inequality and injustice are regular features when you are working and travelling in the developing world.

I heard a worship song recently whose main lyric was *'he gives and he takes away'*. Sometimes it seems that the rich have so much and the poor have so little, and it is hard to take. But ultimately, all things belong to God and he will hold everyone accountable for how they use their possessions.

In this chapter we learn how Nebuchadnezzar the king finally comes to worship God. He has a startling dream about a tree that is destroyed. Daniel reveals to the king that his dream is about himself and that he will be stripped of his glory and sent into the wilderness (v25). However, to his folly, Nebuchadnezzar rejects the interpretation of the dream and pays no attention to it. This was because he did not want to acknowledge anyone greater than himself (v30). It is at this point that everything changes for Nebuchadnezzar. He is driven into the wilderness, just as the dream prophesied, his sanity is taken from him, and he is forced to live with the animals (v33). Then after a long time, he finally acknowledges God as the Most High and his sanity is restored.

There is both a personal and a general lesson in this. None of us should ever be tempted to become high and mighty, because God has his own ways of bringing us to our senses. And we should not be overawed, discouraged or bitter about the rich, powerful and unscrupulous of the world. Their works are all known to God and he deals with them in his own time.

PRAYER & ACTION

- Prayfully read through Philippians 2: 1 - 10 asking that he might help you follow the example of the One who set the ultimate example in humility.

All things belong to God and he will hold everyone accountable for how they use their possessions.

God transforms even the most unlikely of characters

Douglas Noble warns about pride

BIBLE REF:
Daniel 1: 1, 2, 12
3: 13
4: 30 - 37

BIBLE VERSE:
At the end of that time, I, Nebuchadnezzar, raised my eyes toward heaven, and my sanity was restored.

In many ways Nebuchadnezzar the king epitomises the attitude of our generation. Taking pride in his own ability to manage his affairs, he put himself first. Instead of attributing his success to his Maker and worshipping him, he became inflated with pride. Our culture encourages us to think 'I believe in myself, I can do it'. Confidence in our own ability to deal with all the affairs of our lives is instilled into us. Everything in our culture encourages self-promotion, self-assertion, and self-reliance.

It took God to humble Nebuchadnezzar, in ways he could never have foreseen, that eventually brought him to his senses. Sometimes, the unheralded arrival of the harsh realities of life into an otherwise untroubled existence causes great soul searching and may begin the journey of faith. This was Nebuchadnezzar's experience and he summarises his experience in one of the great personal testimonies of all time - *'[All] those who walk in pride, [God] is able to humble'* (4: 37). When you encounter proud, difficult and ruthless people, like Nebuchadnezzar as he used to be, think of this.

Never underestimate the power of God's Spirit to convict people of their sin and bring them to faith (see John 16: 8 - 11). Although we should respect and pray for those who hold high office in the world, we should never be overawed by them. God can bring them very low indeed if they abuse their mandate.

And each of us should be careful not to fall into the same trap as Nebuchadnezzar. It is easy to ignore God when he is closest to us, and be driven into the experience of desolation. God wants us to respond to him through the Cross of Christ, where all pride ends and repentance begins. Nebuchadnezzar eventually realised that all the signs in his life, the dreams and the miracles, pointed to the one true God. And the same is true of the circumstances of your life and mine. If you don't know him, he wants to know you. He loves you and through the Cross of Christ invites you to respond.

> Never underestimate the power of God's Spirit to convict people of their sin and bring them to faith.

PRAYER & ACTION

- Ask God to help you live an example of true love and humility towards others. Ask him for the opportunity to bring the cross of Christ into your conversations today.
- Use the words of John 16: 8 - 11 to pray for any proud, difficult or ruthless people known to you.

Have I not commanded you?
Be strong and courageous.
Do not be terrified, do not be
discouraged, for the Lord
your God will be with you
wherever you go.

Joshua 1:9

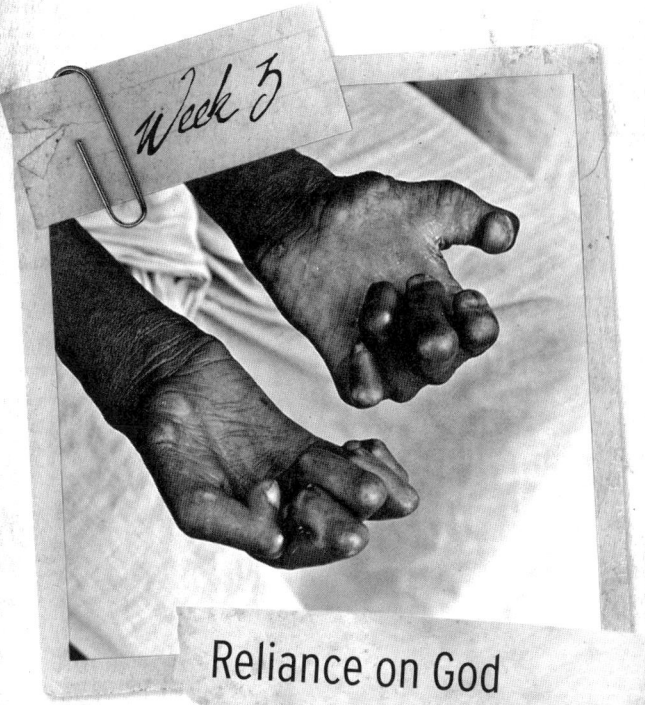

Week 3

Reliance on God

Reliant on God: peace

Claire Hollingsworth tells the story of a prison visit on her Zambian elective

BIBLE REF:
Psalm 29: 11

BIBLE VERSE:
The Lord gives strength to his people, the Lord blesses his people with peace.

It was a Tuesday morning, and as with every day of the six weeks, bright sun streamed through the bedroom window. This morning however, I felt anything but sunny. I was apprehensive and nervous, because today we were visiting the maximum-security prison in Kabwe, and more specifically the condemned men's section. We travelled the short journey to the prison and stepped through a small wooden door in the huge reinforced wooden gates.

Despite having grown accustomed (at least to some degree) to the prisons (having visited about 12 by this stage) today was different. I was about to meet 260 men on death row, and I was scared. My heart still slightly quickens now at the thought of it, but then it was positively trying to escape my rib cage! All sorts of questions flooded my mind - Why was I here? What good could we do? I called out silently to God, 'Father, please give me peace' - and he did. And what's more - I'll never forget that day, and I'll never forget the Christians there. Men who sang with all their hearts, '*my home is not here on earth, but in heaven*'.

That day I remember as if it were yesterday. I had to accept that I couldn't go on without God intervening and stilling my heart, giving me the strength to go on and step over the threshold. So many times it's easy to think we have everything under control, that we can take things in our stride - ride the waves, dodge the storms - but I'm sure God would rather we trusted him in everything, not just in crises!

I called out silently to God, 'Father, please give me peace' - and he did.

PRAYER & ACTION
■ Spend a moment asking God what he'd have you trust in him for, today. Then let him give you his peace for whatever that need is.

Reliant on God: provision

Claire writes about God's provision in a dangerous situation

BIBLE REF:
Genesis 22: 14

BIBLE VERSE:
So Abraham called that place The Lord Will Provide.

It was the end of the six weeks of my elective - and after a very healthy trip, two of our team members became ill, one of them particularly seriously and both requiring hospital admission. Naturally we were concerned for them, and had to delay our proposed travel arrangements until they were discharged.

Unfortunately in order to be able to catch our flight this meant travelling at night (with eight white women in a minibus, and African roads, this already was not an ideal situation) ... and then we started to run short of petrol. Town followed town with no sign of the welcoming green and yellow lights of a BP garage, the tank was on empty and our sick ones needed rest... and so we prayed. A lot! (and then a bit more for good measure). Lo and behold, against all odds, an open petrol station. Coincidence? ... I don't think so!

God is so faithful in providing for our needs and yet it is so easy to forget to thank him for the many things we take for granted in everyday life (OK it sounds cheesy ... but hang on). Sometimes it's only when faced with a situation like the one above, when we're lacking mobile phones or the AA, that we realise how vulnerable we are.

When was the last time we thanked God for keeping us safe as we travel, in my case around the streets of London? I'm not sure I can remember. Perhaps we need to take time to think and recall the many things that God provides us with. Because they are exactly that - his provisions.

PRAYER & ACTION

■ Is prayer a last resort? Start a habit of making prayer your first course of action.

God is so faithful in providing for our needs and yet it is so easy to forget to thank him.

Reliant on God: purpose

**Claire Hollingsworth reminds us
to be faithful in working for God**

So many frustrations, everything so short-term, inappropriate drugs, unjust systems, appalling conditions - so many things counting against being able to make a tangible difference. Yet, a smile, a handshake, a friendly word, a reassuring gesture - and the enormous privilege of sharing the gospel and God's compassion with so many people.

Know what I mean?! It's so easy even in short-term mission work to get bogged down with the difficulties and problems with trying to help people. And so easy to lose perspective on the more important things. It's easy to get frustrated because you move on so quickly that you don't get to see anything completed, or see whether God has worked in the lives of people with whom you've been in contact, or whether prayers you have prayed for specific people have been answered.

The enormous privilege of sharing the gospel and God's compassion with so many people.

ACTION
Read the verse above again and take heart. Refocus, readjust, be rejuvenated ... and *'give yourself fully to the work of the Lord'*.

Everything in good time

Gareth Payne describes how his elective went according to God's plan, not his

BIBLE REF:
Proverbs 3: 5

BIBLE VERSE:
Trust in the Lord with all your heart and lean not on your own understanding.

I was expected to perform a study whilst on elective, but as so often happens outside the West, the pace at which things were done was less than could be hoped. The slow cogs of the bureaucratic machine had to creak into action before I could gain permission to start the data collection in the government hospitals. In fact, I had to wait until the eighth and final week before I could even take a peek at the records!

During that time, many prayers had been said by myself and by some Christians whom I had met whilst out there. God was faithful and our patience was rewarded. However, God had greater plans for me than collecting data for a small study, and I was showered with opportunities I would not otherwise have had, if I'd been sat in an office looking at records. I saw gross pathology, shared my faith, attended clinic outreach, taught English at the local university and formed close relationships with the local CMF students. I met more people and served God in ways I would not have felt possible before my elective. Looking back I know that my elective was a time of increasing my medical confidence, but more importantly it was a time of pushing the boundaries of my comfort zone and served as a crash-course in Christian witnessing and outreach.

It is not always possible to know what God's plan is for us. He answers our prayers, but it would be wise not to limit him. He wants what is good for you and knows the desires of your heart. However, we must be aware that often what we ask for is puny in relation to what God has in store for us and if only we let him, his power will blow our minds.

Remember - Everything in God's Time.

It is not always possible to know what God's plan is for us. He wants what is good for you and knows the desires of your heart.

FURTHER READING
Matthew 7: 7 - 12
Luke 12: 22 - 31
Ecclesiastes 3: 1 - 8

When Christians go it alone

Liz Croton found an unexpected mission field on her elective

BIBLE REF:
Matthew 5: 16

BIBLE VERSE:
Let your light shine before men, that they may see your good deeds and praise your Father in heaven.

I was a young Christian and for my medical elective, I had set my mind on working with a Christian organisation and influencing lives for Christ! Sadly my plans became little more than an ideal when all of my applications were rejected, in the majority of cases due to unforeseen circumstances. I was gutted and resigned myself to what I felt was the second best option - a placement in the Caribbean with six other people, all non-Christians. I was terrified at the prospect of having to be a witness to the rest of the group through my own rather immature Christian faith.

All seven of us were friends but we had widely differing ideals. It became apparent that our trip was to involve large amounts of time drinking rum, smoking hash and visiting strip joints! I couldn't understand why I, in particular, was being sent into such a minefield.

On closer reflection, I realised that Christian mission is not restricted to those employed as 'missionaries'. It is something that we are all called to do wherever we are (Matthew 28: 19 - 20). It reminded me very much of Jesus sending out the twelve like sheep amongst wolves (Matthew 10: 16). I had a tremendous opportunity amongst my friends if I could get alongside them (1 Corinthians 9: 19 - 23).

On the advice of a wise friend, I tracked down a church in the local area beforehand via the Internet and made contact with them. This was a source of great support and a number of Christians made friends with our party.

It was also reassuring that a number of the staff in our placement clinic were committed Christians and great witnesses. I also, following prayer, was able to join in with the party's activities while drawing the line at certain things I felt uncomfortable with. On our return, I felt very strongly that God had softened their hearts towards the Gospel and a number of them started to attend Alpha courses.

This just goes to show that wherever we find ourselves overseas, we can and must make an impact for Christ. Take heart that we have the greatest resource of all - the Holy Spirit - who *helps us in our weakness* (Romans 8: 26).

> I was terrified at the prospect of having to be a witness to the rest of the group.

FURTHER READING
Read the passages in the text in their context.

Spirit-inspired speech

Liz Croton describes how God used her when her own resources had run dry

BIBLE REF:
Jeremiah 1: 6

BIBLE VERSE:
'Ah Sovereign Lord,' I said, 'I do not know how to speak for I am only a child.'

Many Christians serving abroad will have found themselves in situations where they have been asked to teach either in a professional or biblical capacity. While a great privilege, there are times when the going is anything but easy. People may feel inadequate or perhaps under-qualified at taking on something they would not normally get involved in at home.

Such was the case with me. I was three weeks post qualifying as a doctor and still awaiting my GMC certificate when I was invited to run medical seminars and address 100+ students at a Christian medical camp in Central Asia. The majority of them were non-believers, having been brought up in the Communist era. It became rapidly apparent that my audience were expecting me to be the fountain of all knowledge regarding Western medicine when in reality I was a grown-up medical student.

I felt very much like Jeremiah when he was called as prophet. He was tongue-tied and inexperienced but the Lord recognised this and helped him (Jeremiah 1: 7 - 8). In fact, as Christians, we have a tremendous promise that God will ultimately uphold us in all that we do (Isaiah 28: 16, Psalm 55: 22).

The medical seminars were popular and three sessions quickly extended into ten as demand exceeded supply. I was exhausted by mid-week, and a combination of culture shock and tiredness made me really quite unwell. The evening talk I had to give was aptly titled 'depression', which quite succinctly summed up how I felt. The locals tried to comfort me but the language barrier just made me long for home.

When the night came, I was tempted to back out but suddenly became aware of how weak and vulnerable Jesus' disciples were when they set out on their mission. In particular I thought of Paul with his 'thorn' (2 Corinthians 12: 7 - 10) and his insistence that his words demonstrated the Spirit's power through his personal weakness (also please see 1 Corinthians 2: 1 - 5). I was acutely aware of the presence of God during the talk. And later, as I shared how I had felt, many of those present understood what had kept me going and saw something of the Lord Jesus. Never forget the witness we can be to others through times of trial.

> I was acutely aware of the presence of God.

PRAYER & ACTION
Commit to God in prayer your plans for the coming week.

Confess your weakness to him and ask him to give you strength for all your work and activity.

Qualities a missionary needs to display

Alan Vogt explains some of the qualities we need to serve God in a different culture

BIBLE REF:
Ezekiel 3: 15

BIBLE VERSE:
I sat where they sat.
(Authorised Version)

Ezekiel, the prophet, was living with the Israelite exiles in captivity in Babylon, sharing their feelings, far away from home. That verse illustrates four qualities the man of God had in a cross-cultural situation.

Identification:
Coming alongside the people to understand their feelings; being careful in our manner and clothing. For example, exposing too much flesh - by either gender - causes offence in some areas. Cultural sensitivity is needed.

Adaptability:
Adjusting to national customs, with no feelings of superiority. Learning some of the language - even if it is only the greetings - helps to break down the barriers and indicates you are reaching out to them. Go out with the attitude of servanthood. One practical matter - the smells! They are not conveyed in the missionary films or slides. I know of some going out for the first time who are overcome with nausea, facing the odours on the ward from septic sores, etc.

Flexibility:
Early rising may be the order of the day, when it is cooler. Modes of travel may be long, tedious and uncomfortable. Getting used to local food is an ordeal for some, unwilling to give up their favourite ice cream or whatever for several weeks!

A sense of urgency and zeal:
A Bible story that illustrates this further quality is found in 2 Kings 7: 3 - 11, '*This is a day of good news ... Let's go at once and report this*' (v9). It is the story of the four men with leprosy who went over to the Aramean camp and found it deserted, with food and clothing left in abundance. They realised their responsibility to share these things with the starving people of Samaria. We in the West who have so much must be willing to share the Good News readily with those in need.

Let us learn lessons from that missionary ideal, the apostle Paul, in his attitude when taking the Gospel to the Thessalonians. In 1 Thessalonians 2 is a man who is: courageous (v2), no impure motives (v3), a steward of the gospel entrusted to him (v4), not looking for popularity (v5), wholeheartedly involved - 'sharing our lives' (v8), in toil and hardship - not an overseas holiday! (v9), showing over all a genuine loving concern for the people (v8).

Identification, adaptability, flexibility and a sense of urgency and zeal.

PRAYER & ACTION
Spend some time reading and praying through 1 Thessalonians 2 asking the Lord Jesus to equip you for all the work he has called you to. (Ephesians 4: 11-13)

Seek first his kingdom and his righteousness, and all these things will be given to you as well.

Matthew 6:33

Back to basics

Foundations of faith I

Douglas Fishlock asks who Jesus is

BIBLE REF:
Matthew 16: 13 - 20

BIBLE VERSE:
Simon Peter answered, 'You are the Christ, the Son of the living God.'

Who is Jesus? This is the most important question we can ever answer. The disciples were challenged to face this by Jesus himself. Is he an ordinary man or a brilliant religious teacher? Is he a prophet from God or is he something else entirely unexpected? Peter declared that Jesus is the Anointed One, the Son of the living God and Jesus completely approved of this answer. This man Jesus has a unique relationship with God the Father. Jesus told the crowd in Jerusalem:

'*You are from below; I am from above. You are of this world, I am not of this world*' (John 8: 23). The uniqueness of Christ is divisive, for there are so many who want to believe that all religions lead to God. Not so, says Jesus, '*I am the way and the truth and the life. No-one comes to the Father except through Me*' (John 14: 6). Like Peter we must make sure of our foundations. Is Jesus the very heart and soul of our Christian faith? Is Jesus the reason for our Christian service? Does our church membership hinder or enhance our faith in Christ?

We must not add things to our faith that get in the way of serving Christ. We must not dilute the message, for Jesus is the only hope for the world. Jesus not only approved of Peter's answer, he declared that it was inspired by God the Father. In all our difficulties, trials and failures we must hold on tightly to the Lord Jesus. We must trust him in all things and remember that he said:

My sheep listen to My voice; I know them, and they follow Me. I give them eternal life, and they shall never perish; no-one can snatch them out of My hand. (John 10: 27 - 28)

> Who is Jesus? This is the most important question we can ever answer.

PRAYER
Lord Jesus, let me confirm my faith in You, the Son of God, the Saviour of the world. Help me to trust You in every circumstance of my life. Rescue me in temptation and please hold me.

Foundations of faith II

Douglas Fishlock underlines how vital God's word is for our lives

BIBLE REF:
Matthew 7: 21 - 29

BIBLE VERSE:
Not everyone who says to me, 'Lord, Lord,' will enter the kingdom of heaven, but only he who does the will of My Father who is in heaven.

Jesus makes it clear to his disciples that obedience is the key to the faithful Christian life. Just calling him 'Lord' but not obeying the Father gets us nowhere. Such an attitude is like building a house on sand. The foundation is useless and the house will not survive the storm. The person who hears the words of Jesus and puts them into practice is like a man who builds his house on the rock. You should notice an important connection between 'the words of Christ' and the idea of 'building on the rock'.

Throughout the Old Testament faithful Israelites called the Lord God their Rock, for example, the Song of Moses (Deuteronomy 32), Hannah's prayer (1 Samuel 2), and David's Song of Praise (2 Samuel 22). Sixteen psalms declare that God is 'The Rock' and there are many other references. Jesus was claiming the prerogatives of God. The foundation in life you need is God himself and Jesus assures us that obedience to his words does indeed give us that foundation. His words are the very words of God so it is not surprising to hear Jesus say, *'heaven and earth will pass away, but My words will never pass away'* (Matthew 24: 35). What man can claim such indestructibility for his words? Obedience and love go hand in hand as far as our relationship with Jesus is concerned.

Jesus said, *'If anyone loves me, he will obey my teaching. My Father will love him, and we will come to him and make our home with him'* (John 14: 23). What a promise!

There can be no doubt therefore that the words of Christ are the most important words we can ever hear. They are the highest authority for the Christian. So the question must be asked: Do we regularly listen to the word of God and test our actions and motives by it? The ultimate storm of life is the coming judgment of God, and there is no escape from disaster unless our lives are built on the firm foundation of faith in Jesus Christ the Lord.

> The words of Christ are the most important words we can ever hear.

PRAYER
Heavenly Father, give me the power to lay aside worldly ideas and motives and to obey Your Son in every part of my life. I ask in the name of Jesus. Amen.

Foundations of faith III

A reminder that we need to give God our very best if we are to live lives that please him

Paul tells the converted Corinthians to make sure that they are building their lives and fellowship upon secure foundations. He says, '*no-one can lay any foundation other than the one already laid, which is Jesus Christ*' (1 Corinthians 3: 11). But he goes on to warn them that there is a right way and a wrong way to build on this foundation.

This passage in Paul's letter is about the judgment of a Christian's life and work. Certainly the true Christian can only have one foundation - that is Jesus Christ the Lord - but he can build 'the house' of his life and work in two different ways. He can use top quality material such as gold, silver and precious stones, or he can use substandard items such as wood, hay or straw. These perishable materials will in no way survive the 'fire of judgment'. The coming of the Lord in judgment is often likened to a fire. Malachi says, '*Who can endure the day of his coming? ... For he will be like a refiner's fire*' (Malachi 3: 2).

Paul makes it quite clear that he is not talking about gaining or losing salvation (v15). What is on trial is the quality of the building the Christian has constructed. '*If what he has built survives, he will receive his reward*' (v14). What this says to me is that I should put my very best into my Christian life. The best of my time and effort are to be spent on my Christian service - once my life is secure upon the foundation of faith in Christ the Lord. I wish someone had explained that to me when I was younger. How much effort have I expended on things that in the light of the Gospel are worthless and will not stand the test of time or the searching, refining fires of God's judgment? For the love of Christ we should use the best of materials to build and maintain our Christian lives and service. Our churches and fellowships, in like manner, must receive the best support that we can give. Are we determined to do this?

> We should use the best of materials to build and maintain our Christian lives and service.

PRAYER
Help me, heavenly Father, to review my Christian life and service in the light of Your holy word. Help me to get my priorities right and to put Christ first. In his name. Amen.

Foundations of faith IV

Douglas Fishlock shows that lives built
on good foundations should lead
others to Jesus

BIBLE REF:
1 Peter 2: 4 - 10

BIBLE VERSE:
See, I lay a
stone in Zion,
a chosen and
precious
cornerstone,
and the one
who trusts in
him will never
be put to
shame.

The church as a fellowship of Christ's people has a distinctive purpose on earth. Peter tells us that as we come to Christ as individuals we are built together into a spiritual house for the service of God. The cornerstone was used as the foundation and orientation of an ancient building. The Messiah is called the 'Cornerstone' in the Old Testament (Psalm 118 and Isaiah 28), and Jesus picks up this theme in the Parable of the Tenants (Matthew 21: 33 - 45). Peter reminds us that this Stone causes people to stumble. Jesus is a 'Rock of offence' because men and women cannot or will not admit that he is Lord.

Peter directs us to Jesus; his letter is full of who Jesus is and what he has done for us. He tells his readers that whatever their background, they have become a chosen people, a royal priesthood and a holy nation. So it is for us; once we were not God's people but now in Christ we belong to God and this is for a purpose that we may declare to the world the praises of him who called us out of darkness into his wonderful light. There is no more important work in this world than the declaration of the Gospel of Christ.

Of course we must care for the sick and feed the hungry but all this is of no avail unless they hear that Jesus died to save them. We may not be preachers but we must take into account the most important need that people have. They need to experience the forgiveness of God and we should pray, as we serve, that the light of the Gospel will come to those whom we help. We should speak out about our faith but be careful to seek God's time and opportunity. We may need to 'earn' the right to tell people the truth. We may need to love them and serve them to win their acceptance before the opportunity comes, but we must never stop seeking to declare the love of God for lost men, women and children.

There is no more important work in this world than the declaration of the Gospel of Christ.

PRAYER

Lord God, help me to serve You in whatever way You have decided. Help me to love people for Your sake and to seek to alleviate their greatest need by introducing them to Jesus. In his name. Amen.

Seek first the kingdom

Peggy Burton encourages us to trust in God's provision and live for him

BIBLE REF:
Matthew 6: 33
Daniel 4: 3

BIBLE VERSE:
Seek first his Kingdom and his Righteousness, and all these things will be given to you as well.

Jesus is talking to his disciples and the people who really want to listen to what he has to say. He has been instructing them, warning them against undisciplined and unfavourable behaviour, following up the teaching of the Beatitudes. In all his teaching he emphasises the element of love and concern they should have for others. He also emphasises their unnecessary and constant tendency to worry and be concerned. In conclusion, he commands them to look to the glories of the Kingdom, and to listen to him. In doing this, the things they have been so worried about will all sort themselves out. But they must listen to him.

Even the most spiritually minded of us tend to consider the necessities of life before considering the Kingdom of God. I must eat; I must be clothed; I must make money; I must get a job, etc. Are you anxious about such things? But our Lord said, '*do not worry about your life...*' (Matthew 6: 25). This does not mean that you neglect your life and let your standards drop, for this would mean neglecting the Temple of the Holy Spirit. '*Do you not know that your body is a temple of the Holy Spirit, who is in you, whom you have received from God? You are not your own*' (1 Corinthians 6: 19).

No, Jesus meant that you should make your relationship with God the dominating factor in your life, and everything else should take second place. Get your priorities right and God will see to it that everything else will be taken care of and you will then have no cause to worry.

> Get your priorities right and God will see to it that everything else will be taken care of.

PRAYER & ACTION
Spend some time prayerfully meditating on the Beatitudes (Matthew 5: 1 - 12) and on the Lord's Prayer (Matthew 6: 9 - 15).

Worship in the kingdom

Steve Fouch takes a fresh look at what worship really means

BIBLE REF:
Isaiah 58: 1 - 12

BIBLE VERSE:
Is this not the fast which I choose; to loosen the bonds of wickedness, to undo the bands of the yoke, and to let the oppressed go free... is it not to divide your bread with the hungry, and bring the homeless poor into your house?

(New American Standard Version)

There is much that is written about worship these days. So many worship CDs, so many high profile worship leaders and new songs and songwriters appearing all the time. Some people choose their churches on the basis of how 'good' the worship is. We have become consumers of worship - it is now an industry worth thousands if not million of pounds (or dollars) every year. While not wishing to decry the intent behind most of this (which is, I believe all ultimately aimed at God's glory), when I come to verses like this one (and I would add Isaiah 1: 11 - 17 & Jeremiah 7: 3 - 6), I wonder if we are missing the point sometimes?

God, speaking through Isaiah, shows how fed up he was with empty worship that ignored justice. For while they fasted, sacrificed, held festivals and so forth, these worshippers exploited their workers, let people go hungry and denied the poor and the vulnerable justice. How much are we in the West guilty of the same things today?

In our world we can often be blind to the inequalities that exist. One of the hardest things about working in the developing world is that you come up against the cold, heartless reality of the injustice and inequality that surround you. It can be a brutal awakening for us, and may make us feel guilty that so much of what we have at home has been bought off the suffering backs of the poor. And in truth, much of it has.

But God, being merciful, does not leave things with condemnation. He would rather see one person saved than cast into hell, and he shows us the response he is looking for. It is a sacrificial response - to care for the weak, feed the hungry and give shelter and clothing to the homeless and naked (even at the cost of giving up our own food and clothing and opening up our own homes). It is the costly way, but the fruits outweigh the costs - '*Then your light will rise in the darkness and your gloom will become like midday*' (v10b). Justice is a part of true worship, true joy and the fruit of the Kingdom of heaven. In the topsy-turvy economy of the Kingdom of God, the more we give away, the more we receive (Mark 8: 35 - 36).

This is the challenge of healthcare mission - to care for the poor and oppressed. Those alongside whom you are now working have responded to that need and the cry from God's heart to act justly. Ask any of them and they'll tell you the cost they've paid. But I'd bet my bottom dollar that they will, in the same breath, tell you of the wonderful things he has done since they responded to that call. That is the true power and joy of worship in the Kingdom of heaven.

In the topsy-turvy economy of the Kingdom of God, the more we give away, the more we receive.

PRAYER & ACTION
Meditate on these verses and pray that God would open your eyes day by day to how you can act justly and worship him in truth in your work, your home, and your church.

Let's have a time of worship

Janet Goodall shows that worship is a way of life

BIBLE REF:
Psalm 95: 6

BIBLE VERSE:
Come, let us bow down in worship.

A Ugandan child cured of meningitis, and prompted by her grandmother, embarrassingly knelt at my feet. People often knelt, bowed or threw themselves down before Jesus, sometimes in expectation or gratitude, usually in worship (Matthew 15: 25; 2: 11; 28: 9). In the Old Testament too, worshippers bowed down in awe to God (Genesis 24: 26; Exodus 4: 31; Psalm 99: 5).

Whereas Scripture often links praise to God with joyful music and singing, worship is rarely mentioned in this context. It usually indicates reverence and submission (hence bowing down), and is first mentioned by Abraham on his way to offer up Isaac (Genesis 22: 5). Paul also urges us *'to offer your bodies as living sacrifices'*, defining this as *'your spiritual act of worship'* (Romans 12: 1). The Greek words for worship and service have the same root, so that true worshippers are faithful servants of God, whatever the cost involved, and not always to the sound of music.

After our fervent songs of praise as part of a Sunday service, what happens on Monday? We may not feel so inspired when the clinic runs on past mealtime, or when everyone else disappears and leaves us to cope alone, or when a patient dies and the relatives want to see us. Even so, we can offer all these (and sterner) trials up to God. He knows how hard it can be to keep going, but his self-giving love will encourage and enable our self-giving in return. This does not exclude a song of praise, even when we don't really feel like it (Acts 16: 25). It is though, our day-to-day service submitted to God, which recalls to him the *aroma of Christ* - and **that** came from his personal sacrifice for us (2 Corinthians 2: 15; Ephesians 5: 2).

A 'wholehearted time of worship' should last a lifetime and our Lord's final 'Well done!' will make it all worthwhile (Matthew 25: 19 - 21).

A 'wholehearted time of worship' should last a lifetime!

PRAYER & ACTION
Use Psalm 95 as the basis for a time of prayer and meditation.

Why not try and memorise part or all of Psalm 95? You could learn a small section each day by writing 2 or 3 verses on a card to keep in your pocket which you could then refer to when you have a few spare moments.

Where, O death, is your victory?
Where, O death, is your sting?
The sting of death is sin,
and the power of sin is the law.
But thanks be to God!
He gives us the victory through
our Lord Jesus Christ.

1 Corinthians 15:55–57

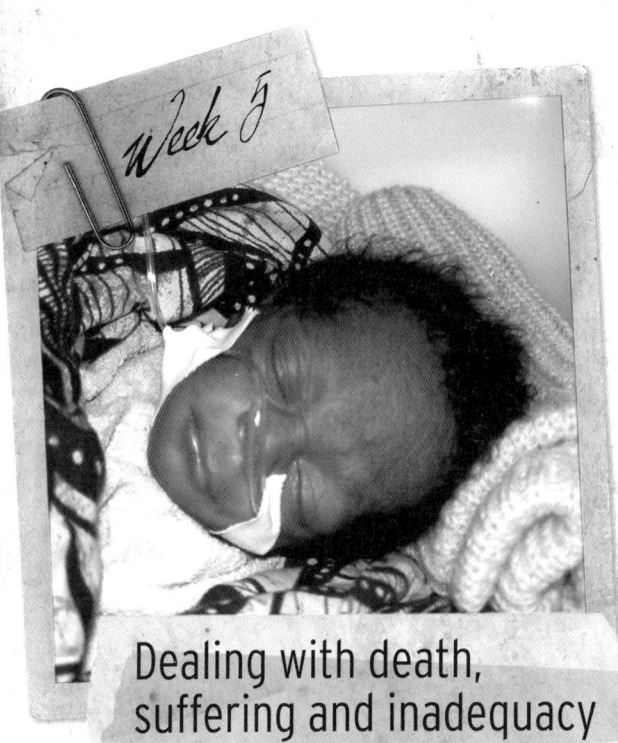

Week 5

Dealing with death,
suffering and inadequacy

Comfort in the face of death

Sally-Ann Jenkins looks at finding God in the midst of suffering, death and grief

BIBLE VERSE:
Praise be to the God and Father of our Lord Jesus Christ, the Father of compassion and the God of all comfort, who comforts us in all our troubles, so that we can comfort those in any trouble with the comfort we ourselves have received from God.

It is very hard, living in the world and rubbing shoulders with worldly values on a daily basis, to keep ourselves pure and unaffected. We're quick to rely on ourselves, look to ourselves for strength and to look to ourselves for answers. When we do turn to God in times of helplessness it is easy to relate to him as the world does - asking why but not really expecting any answers.

How quickly we forget the enormity of God's arms, the extent of his compassion and the depths of his knowledge and love. He knows our needs even before we do.

Paul, when facing the sentence of death, was reminded again of the need to be fully reliant on God - to express that childlike trust that comes of knowing that there is nothing that we can do ourselves and that we are completely in the hands of Another. Yet how glorious to know that the One in whom we put our trust is the God who raises the dead. Paul and his companions could have complete confidence that if they met their earthly death they would be raised to eternal life. They could also have complete confidence that the Creator of the heavens and earth was fully able to save them from such deadly peril as they faced. He can deliver, he has delivered and he will continue to deliver from death now and eternally.

Prayer is effective and powerful. Paul was confident that, in response to prayers as yet unarticulated, God will continue to save. He hears our prayers and responds with gracious favour. When faced with our own helplessness in the face of death, what a comfort to know that there is One to whom we can pray - who will hear our prayers and who has the ability to save.

However, we mustn't think that we can bend God's will to ours. We must also have something of the perspective of Esther. She prayed and fasted in the face of almost certain death, and the company of Jews prayed and fasted with her. She knew God to be a rescuing God, but also knew that he was in control, that our ways are often far from his and she was prepared to trust him absolutely in life and death. She was praying for rescue (which came!) but without any sense of personal or sovereign failure if she died. God was in control 'and if I perish, I perish' was her response.

Facing death causes us to 'rely not on ourselves but on God' (v9), and enables us to both experience and pass on the comfort of the God and Father of our Lord Jesus Christ. We are reminded of his power to defeat death, to raise the dead and to do immeasurably more than all we ask or imagine. We are reminded of the love that sent Christ to the cross and that can never be taken away from us. We are reminded that in Christ we have an Intercessor who has had experience of living in a fallen world and is well able to sympathise with our needs. We are reminded that God knows our needs and is delighted to meet them in response to prayer - others' and ours. And we are reminded that this comfort is ours to pass on to others, so that they also may set their hope on God, who raises the dead.

> How quickly we forget the enormity of God's arms, the extent of his compassion and the depths of his knowledge and love.

Our response to death and suffering

Sally-Ann Jenkins writes about hope in the face of death

BIBLE REF:
John 11: 1 - 43

BIBLE VERSE:
When Jesus saw her weeping, and the Jews who had come along with her also weeping, he was deeply moved in spirit and troubled. 'Where have you laid him?' he asked. 'Come and see, Lord' they replied. Jesus wept.

When it touches us, death leaves us confused and hurting. We feel a sense of inadequacy as we sit by the elderly and watch their lives slip away - whether it is in peace or pain, we mourn for the gap that their passing leaves in the world, and our inability to hold onto their presence just a little longer. When the young die we feel a sense of injustice and the pain is raw. Why could we not protect this life? Why did God allow this to happen?

Death strips away all our defences and pretensions - we are not in control. It is even more poignant when we know that if we had the resources or technology to hand then we could have saved this life. Our helplessness leaves us feeling so angry.

Mary must have felt so many of these emotions as she watched her brother die, but then on top of this was the sense of having been failed by her Lord and Friend - if Jesus had been there this would not have happened. Who can imagine the turmoil of her emotions as Jesus appears on the scene four days later? Yet when he comes he does so in compassion, with real depth of feeling, and not four days too late as we might at first think, but right on time to demonstrate God's glory.

Death is a hard reminder to us all that we have rejected God, and Jesus is deeply moved in spirit and troubled by the very presence of death in the world. Death was the consequence of rejecting God in Genesis 2: 17, and is a deeply painful reminder to God of the rebelliousness of his creation as he watches that which he created to be pleasing and good,

WEEK 5
DAY 30

suffer, face pain and die. It is right that we should feel a sense of anger and outrage over death - it is not part of God's good creation and has no part in his glorious recreation (Revelation 21: 4). It is right that we should feel impotent in the face of death - to remember that ultimate authority and control are God's and not ours. It is right that we should weep and mourn with the grieving and at the presence of death - Jesus wept as he stood by the grave of his friend.

But it is also right that we should remember that death is also just a gateway through which we must all pass. Physical death is inescapable, but there is a life beyond it. How prepared are we for what comes beyond physical death? Jesus demonstrates not only his control over death, but also his victory as he raises his friend Lazarus back to life and in his own resurrection from the dead. In both of these Jesus confirms his claim that he is the resurrection and the life. That whoever believes in him will live even though he dies, and that whoever lives and believes in him will never die (John 11: 25 - 26).

It is right to feel the pain of death, but there is a glorious hope for all who trust in Christ - that death is not the end, but the gateway to eternal life.

> Death strips away all our defences and pretensions - we are not in control.

Where is God?

Sally-Ann Jenkins reminds us of the fragility of life, and God's great goodness to us

BIBLE REF:
Psalm 90

BIBLE VERSE:
Teach us to number our days aright, that we might gain a heart of wisdom.

Living in the West can have a domesticating effect on our understanding of God. As we look up to the skyline we see monuments to man's greatness - we see skyscrapers dwarfing the spires of churches that once dominated a town, and high overhead a jumbo jet proclaims our mastery of the heavens. On the ground we see testament to our progress and to our introspection, as people walk busily past engaged with their mobile phones or palm pilots or iPods. Where in all this is the God who created the heavens and the earth?

Of course he is still there, but it can be hard for us to see him. It can be hard to see beyond our own lives to the God who is from everlasting to everlasting. When we are removed from our protective technological bubbles and forced to see the reality of our frailty, we see what sophistication has hidden from us. Namely that life is so transitory... full of promise one moment and swept out of our hands the next, that death is a reality that comes to us all and that it comes at the hands of a God from whom nothing is hidden. We may try to persuade ourselves that we are 'OK', but God sees our 'secret sins', he knows our iniquities and his wrath is upon us. As the psalmist says, *'Who knows the power of Your anger? For Your wrath is as great as the fear that is due to You'* (v11).

We cannot hide from God's wrath but we do our best to hide the knowledge of his wrath from our eyes. We take refuge in the safety of our world and do not fear the One from whom no secrets are hid. Yet how dangerous and myopic a perspective this is when God can *sweep men away in the sleep of death; they are like the new grass of the morning - though in the morning it springs up new, by evening it is dry and withered'* (vs5 - 6).

However, death re-tunes our vision and reorients us back towards God. Moses goes on to say (in our text above), *'Teach us to number our days aright, that we may gain a heart of wisdom'*. As we contemplate our humble beginnings and our dusty endings we are reminded that God is sovereign, and that he is more awesome and terrifying than we could imagine. We are reminded that death is the penalty we pay for having rejected him and that trouble and sorrow are the hallmarks of living in a fallen world - the fear of the Lord is the beginning of wisdom.

We cannot fear the God we do not know, yet as we get to know him and see his awesome might, so also we know him as our refuge and our dwelling place. There is joy to be found in the sorrow and toil of our fallen lives, for the Lord is compassionate. His love is unfailing, so even though life is full of trouble and strife still, yet his love satisfies us, fills us to the very core. That we may be able to sing for joy and be glad all our days - no mean feat given what we have seen of the depth of his wrath at our sinfulness, and of the tyranny of death. Yet is that not the splendour of the cross? As we look at our own death we are terrified by God's wrath, but as we look at Jesus' death we rejoice at his unfailing love. Death is truly the key to life.

Life is so transitory... full of promise one moment and swept out of our hands the next.

Death conquered

Sally-Ann Jenkins reminds us that Jesus has finally conquered death

BIBLE REF:
Revelation 20: 11 - 15

BIBLE VERSE:
Then death and Hades were thrown into the lake of fire. The lake of fire is the second death. If anyone's name was not found in the book of life he was thrown into the lake of fire.

The prevailing attitudes towards death in the West are either to show a fear of death and the unknown, or conversely to show a contemptuous lack of fear of death and the unknown. The fear of death can be seen in our refusal to talk about it, our refusal to prepare people for it outside of palliative care, the attitude that must call in the specialists if someone has a terminal diagnosis, assuming that it is not something that the ordinary practitioner can really deal well with. We also tend to hide behind the philosophy of treatment at all costs. The lack of fear of death is shown particularly in our attitude towards euthanasia and in what we teach about the purpose of life and the existence of the afterlife.

As Christians we know that both are right responses, but for completely different reasons. It is right to fear death, as this is God's punishment on mankind for its rejection of him as the One with the right to call the shots (not a nice thought but true - see again Genesis 2: 17). In particular it is right to fear death if we are unrepentant for our rejection of God - Jesus' own experience shows us that facing God's wrath in death is greatly to be feared (see Luke 22: 22 - 44). However, we also know that there is now no condemnation for those who are in Christ Jesus (Romans 8: 1). Jesus has set us free from the power of death by dying in our place; because of his sacrifice, the dead shall be raised imperishable (1 Corinthians 15: 52) to spend eternity with God in heaven. There is nothing for the Christian to fear in death.

We need not fear death for ourselves, but the presence of death around us should remind us of the certainty of judgment and the reality of heaven and hell. It should move us towards an urgency to proclaim the gospel. Death is not the end. At the end of time the dead will be raised imperishable. And those who have trusted in Jesus, whose names are found in The Book Of Life, will spend eternity in God's heavenly dwelling place. Whilst those who remain in rebellion will be raised only to face the second death - eternal separation from God in a place of wailing and gnashing of teeth. Jesus' resurrection proclaims both his victory over death, and also the certainty of judgment (Acts 17: 31).

To prepare people for death we need to be telling them the truth about Jesus and his resurrection, in the hope and fervent desire that when they stand before the heavenly throne they might be found among those whose names are written in the Book of Life.

> We need not fear death for ourselves, but the presence of death around us should remind us of the certainty of judgment and the reality of heaven and hell.

The problem of guidance

Alan Vogt writes about finding God's will in our lives

BIBLE REF:
Genesis 24

BIBLE VERSE:
I, being in the way, the Lord led me.

All Christians at any age come across the problem of guidance. What is God's will for me at this time? Let us learn from the story of Abraham's servant, travelling to another country with a specific purpose. He had a tricky task - to find a wife for his master's son, Isaac. We may find it hard to find the right life partner for ourselves - much more difficult for someone else! The three principles he adopted can teach us in whatever circumstances we need guidance. An apt quotation is this: '*The guided man or woman is one who has large thoughts about God*'. As we put God first and honour him, step-by-step, we will be shown the way.

The way of obedience

The servant solemnly promised to obey his master's wishes (v9), and was assured the Lord would go before him to bring him in the right way (v7). What an encouragement to us as we step out into an unknown land! Be sure obedience will be tested with difficulties and opposition.

The way of humble service

The servant was not self-seeking but wholly wanting to carry out the purpose of Abraham, continually calling him 'My Master'. As Christians, we are out to serve our Lord and Master, Jesus Christ. Romans 12 reminds us this involves self-discipline and self-sacrifice, denying our own comforts to be his disciples (Luke 9: 23). '*Love so amazing, so divine, demands my soul, my life, my all*' are the challenging words of Isaac Watts' hymn.

The way of prayer

The whole expectations of the servant were soaked in prayer. '*O LORD, God ... give me success today*' (v12 - NIV). And '*...the man bowed down and worshipped the LORD*' (v26). Many missionaries can look back on their lives and be thankful to see how the various pieces of the jigsaw puzzle have fitted together. If we're going to be successful in the Christian life, we must walk closely with the Lord - starting each day listening to him speaking to us through this word and throughout the day, maintaining an attitude of prayerful trust - in all our ways acknowledging him (Proverbs 3: 5 - 6). We need to be continually filled with his Spirit to understand the Lord's will (Ephesians 5: 15 - 20) - a mind focused on pleasing the Lord. Let us walk in this way, guided by the word of God and the promptings of the Spirit of God within. As someone has said, 'With the word alone, we dry up; with the Spirit alone we blow up; with the word and the Spirit, we grow up!'

> The guided man or woman is one who has large thoughts about God.

PRAYER & ACTION
Use the verses above and also Psalm 32. 8 and Isaiah 30: 21 as a starting point for prayer, committing your future plans to God. Ask him to lead you and guide you according to his will.

Am I accomplishing anything?

Marjory Foyle encourages us that God works mightily through our small gifts

BIBLE REF:
Zechariah 4

BIBLE VERSE:
Who despises the day of small things? People will rejoice when they see a plumb line in the hand of Zerubbabel.

Many of us who work overseas sometimes ask ourselves if we are really accomplishing anything? For cultural reasons we may live without much affirmation, and there is often so much need around us that we feel the tiny drop we are contributing does very little to help.

Do not be disheartened. God has given us a wonderful story in the book of Zechariah that explains how to manage these feelings. An angel saw what a mess Jerusalem was in when the rest of the earth seemed to be doing quite well (Zechariah 1: 11 - 12). He turned to God in deep distress, and almost reproached him for not doing anything about it. God was not angry with him - he saw his distress, and spoke *'kind and comforting words'* to him (Zechariah 1: 13, one of my favourites).

These comforting words were of two kinds. First, God explained that despite Jerusalem being just a heap of rubble, he was actually in control, and was preparing an act of restoration. The second kind was a visual aid. He sent a man to stand in the ruins of the city with a measuring line in his hand (Zechariah 2: 1). The first step in any building project is to do a survey to measure the site. So the use of this line indicated that rebuilding was actually going to happen.

WEEK 5
DAY 34

The point is confirmed later (Zechariah 4: 10), when the plumb line is introduced. Any old-fashioned builder knows that a plumb line, a piece of string with a lead weight on it, was used to find out if the building was straight. God was assuring the Jews that a new Temple was going to arise where the old one had been! The important thing to remember is that although the plumb line was only a little thing, it had a profound meaning, and we should never, never, never forget this:

Who despises the day of small things?
Men will rejoice when they see the plumb line
in the hand of Zerubbabel (Zechariah 4: 10).

This verse kept me going through 30 years of overseas missionary work, and a further twenty years caring for missionary mental health. I used to wonder if I was accomplishing anything, and would remind myself of the Zechariah principle - God never despises the day of small things, for they are done *'Not by might nor by power, but by My Spirit'* (Zechariah 4: 6).

May you be encouraged today as you go about doing 'small things'.

There is often so much need around us that we feel the tiny drop we are contributing does very little to help.

PRAYER & ACTION
Why not take the time to read the first four chapters of Zechariah? Pick out 2 or 3 verses and use them as the basis for prayer.

Ordinary people achieve the extraordinary

Mark Forshaw on how God achieved great things through an ordinary woman

BIBLE REF:
Ruth 1

BIBLE VERSE:
Where you go I will go, and where you stay I will stay. Your people will be my people and your God my God.

The Bible narrative of Ruth is an account of how God uses an ordinary person to perform the extraordinary. And chapter one of Ruth encapsulates this. As we read the chapter, we read of how God used Ruth, a person who at first could seem quite ordinary.

Verses 1 - 5 describe disastrous times of famine, bereavement, widowhood, hunger, and refugees; in a time of war and political instability (Judges 3: 1 - 6). A description all too real for those living and working in the developing world of the 21st Century. When we look at the words of Naomi we see one who is grief stricken and despairing.

In verses 6 - 18 however, God is at work. In verse 6 we read that he sent his word of how he was rescuing people. Naomi decides to return to her people, but again we are not spared her grief and despair expressed towards God. How often today do we hear the cry of HIV positive mothers despairing at the loss of their husbands and at the uncertainty, when they too are gone, of what will happen to their children?

But the account changes with the decision of one person, Ruth (vs16 - 17), to abandon her old gods, to serve Naomi and the one true God, with no going back. The provision of Ruth is God's answer to Naomi's cry for help.

The remainder of the book of Ruth is the account of how Ruth continues to walk alongside Naomi in a serving and faithful manner and of how God blesses Ruth and Naomi. But we also know now that all mankind would be blessed through one of her descendants, Jesus Christ, the perfect example of serving, who *'did not come to be served, but to serve, and to give his life as a ransom for many'* (Mark 10: 45).

And where does Ruth get the strength from to give so much day by day? From her faith (v16), shown in deciding for God. And we see from her prayer in verse 17, *'May the LORD deal with me...'* she knows whom she is following.

Verses 19 - 22 show 'Dependence on God'. Even with the provision of Ruth, Naomi struggles to deal with the crises that she is facing. Just like Job and the psalmist, she pours out her honest feelings of grief - they take God seriously (v20). But again God answers with the provision of the humble daughter in law, Ruth, in verse 22 - where we also see the mention of the barley harvest, an end to famine, a provision from God.

With faith and a serving humble commitment, the seemingly ordinary Ruth performed the extraordinary, not only for Naomi, but also for eternity. By walking alongside people in their times of need, God can perform great things through us all, for his glory.

> When we look at the words of Naomi we see one who is grief stricken and despairing.

I pray that you, being rooted and established in love, may have power, together with all the saints, to grasp how wide and long and high and deep is the love of Christ, and to know this love which surpasses knowledge — that you may be filled to the measure of all the fullness of God.

Ephesians 3:16–19

Week 6

Finding God
where it matters

You are my God

Jenny Wordley reminds us to take time to 'sit at the feet of our Lord'

BIBLE REF:
Psalm 63

BIBLE VERSE:
O God, you are my God, earnestly I seek You.

My dental elective in 1998 was hard work but I loved it. I was working in a school for children living in the slum areas of Mexico City. As a dental student I was attached to the dental clinic, although I quickly realised that I was regarded as the on-hand medical worker with responsibilities for all health care concerns from simple headaches to ingrowing toenails! Two days into my elective and to my great apprehension I was told that I would be giving lessons on health care in Spanish. Having arrived without knowing a single word I struggled desperately to communicate with the children. With a mocked-up giant toothbrush in the form of a modified yard broom, I demonstrated the up and down motion of model tooth brushing technique.

'Up and Cow! Up and Cow!' I yelled out enthusiastically in my best 'espanol' to the great amusement of the children watching this strange '*Dentista*'.

It was a tremendous privilege, a lot of fun and I found myself facing new situations and challenges every day. Differences in culture intrigued me and I realised just how British I can be! To my surprise I discovered that I needed quiet time to myself too - moments of peace and reflection in a busy people-filled schedule.

Sometimes we just need to step away from the rush of activity and behold the Lord:

O God, You are my God,
earnestly I seek You (v1).
Because Your love is better than life (v3).

So often we are rushing from one thing to the next, never stopping to hold the moment and listen to God. Living life at 100mph, 'Martha-ing' it, rather than sitting at the feet of our Lord (Luke 10: 38 - 42). We can live trying to solve all the problems life flings at us, and achieving all those things we **must** get done, but perhaps we are missing the point? It is often when we feel utterly unable to cope that we finally remember to turn to the Lord. It is in these times that we can take heart from the truth of this psalm:

Because You are my help, I sing in
the shadow of Your wings.
My soul clings to You; Your right hand
upholds me. (vs7 - 8)

Perhaps it is then in our honest vulnerability that we stop, listen and look to our Lord.

> Sometimes we just need to step away from the rush of activity and behold the Lord.

PRAYER & ACTION
O God You are my God. In good times and bad, through the easier moments and the tougher times You are my God! I can trust in You to bring me through all my days until I am welcomed home. Amen.

Spiritual vision

Ian Spillman encourages us not to be afraid in the face of opposition

BIBLE REF:
2 Kings 6: 8 - 17

BIBLE VERSE:
'Don't be afraid,' the prophet answered. 'Those who are with us are more than those who are with them.'

We often feel overwhelmed by situations that seem impossible. The king of Aram was furious as his raids into Israel were repeatedly thwarted. Having discovered that Elisha the prophet knows his plans and warns the king of Israel of the raids, he sends *'horses and chariots and a strong force there. They went by night and surrounded the city'* (v14).

Elisha's servant is up early the next morning and sees the overwhelming force arrayed against them - impossible odds humanly speaking. He calls out to Elisha, bewildered, *'what shall we do?'*

Often in our NHS jobs and certainly in missionary medical work, there are times where the demands and pressures seem overwhelming and we too can cry out 'What shall we do?'

I love the peace in Elisha as he reassures his servant, and says: *'Those who are with us are more than those who are with them'*. Humanly it's a ridiculous statement, wishful thinking, and an ostrich-with-head-in-the-sand type of reaction. But Elisha has his spiritual vision and he knows the real situation in the light of eternity.

He prays, therefore, not for himself but for his frightened servant: *'O LORD, open his eyes so he may see'* and God graciously answers, allowing the servant to view what Elisha could already see - the hills full of horses and chariots of fire all around Elisha.

God repeatedly in his word reassures us to 'Fear not'. He says time and time again, *'for I am with you... Nothing can separate you from My love... Be not dismayed for I am your God...'*

Let us pray that our eyes may be opened so, like David, we do not fear the giants but know we are safe with our heavenly Father always with us.

You, dear children, are from God and have overcome them, because the one who is in you is greater than the one who is in the world.
(1 John 4: 4)

PRAYER & ACTION
Commit to God in prayer any seemingly impossible situations that are causing you to worry, thanking God that he is able to give you strength to face them.

Often in our NHS jobs and certainly in missionary medical work, there are times where the demands and pressures seem overwhelming and we too can cry out 'What shall we do?'

Men made new

Ian Spillman writes about the transformation of lives touched by Jesus

BIBLE REF:
Luke 8: 26 - 39

BIBLE VERSE:
**Return home
and tell how
much God has
done for you.**

I was on-call at Kisiizi early one Sunday morning when the watchman banged his spear on our bedroom window to summon me to a man who had been carried unconscious all night across the hills. The team of men from the village who had taken turns carrying the 'helicopter' (a stretcher carried by four men on their heads) now stood peering through the ward windows to see what would happen.

We took him into our treatment room and guessed he might be hypoglycaemic from alcohol the previous evening. After a bolus of IV glucose he started to surface and a couple of minutes later was able to walk back into the ward. I wish I had had a camera to record the looks of astonishment on the faces of those who had laboured so hard to carry him. In fact some began to assume he had been acting and had to be reassured that he had indeed been unwell. It was a dramatic transformation from helplessness to wholeness.

As we read of many of the encounters of Jesus with a whole cross-section of society, we repeatedly see those around him staring in amazement at the transformation he produced, at 'men made new'.

Who, for example, was the first missionary? A devoted follower? A chosen disciple? No, a madman among tombs (See Mark 5: 1 - 20 and then the version in Luke 8: 26 - 39).

The local people did not know how to handle this madman - he broke free from chains and roamed wild, distressed, flailing, screaming and naked in a cemetery.

'Absolutely no good to anyone', they probably said, yet Jesus pilots the boat to land near him. Imagine the reaction of the disciples - gawping, maybe cowering in the boat, horrified... and then their open-mouthed astonishment as the power and compassion of the Saviour transform and restore this precious child of God. He was indeed hopeless until the voice of Jesus was heard, then life was never the same again.

It was an explosive encounter - we see the confidence of Jesus, we catch a glimpse of unseen warfare: 'you evil spirits come out!' Jesus wants this man back. The demons retreat powerless, the disciples stand back and watch the Father fight. And rising from the ashes is the new man, calm and in his right mind, and now given a purpose, a Commission, to share the Good News of this Saviour.

So the man went away and told all over the town how much Jesus had done for him (Luke 8: 39b).

> We repeatedly see those around Jesus staring in amazement at the transformation he produced, at 'men made new'.

PRAYER & ACTION
Spend some time praying for those you've met and for those who you will meet today, asking God to produce new life in their hearts.

Go and sin no more

Mary Hopper writes about the danger of judging others

BIBLE REF:
John 8: 1 - 11

BIBLE VERSE:
'Then neither do I condemn you,' Jesus declared. 'Go now and leave your life of sin.'

The sun rising over the temple courts was casting long shadows in amongst the colonnades where the followers of Jesus were gathered. Some church leaders of the Pharisees' group dragging a young girl behind them suddenly interrupted the teaching session. They proudly announced before the crowd that they had witnessed her committing adultery.

Jesus was well aware that, rather than being concerned about the sexual life of this young woman or their responsibilities to uphold the law, the Pharisees were intent on placing him in a position where they could accuse him of breaking the law.

It looked impossible. If he judged that they should follow the teaching of Moses and have the girl stoned to death, he would be contravening the law of the occupying Roman forces. Yet if he suggested anything other than that, it would be interpreted that he was unwilling to uphold God-given law.

What must the woman have felt like? She had apparently been caught in the very act of adultery - in bed with a man who was not her husband. She must surely have been shaking in fear as she watched her accusers gathering stones for her execution. She may also have been contemplating the shame she would be bringing upon her family and friends, as well as that which she felt as she was paraded before the crowd.

'What do You say? Answer us!' they yelled. 'Shall we stone her?'

Eventually and in his time he gave them a look, which totally demolished them - he looked them in the eye! The law stated that anyone who had witnessed the sin should commence the execution by throwing the first stones; but immediately Jesus challenged them to first consider their own hearts.

How differently we can view the sins of others when we see them through the murky waters of our own past.

Those who came with the headlines '*this woman was caught in the act*' crept away with their heads bowed trying to dispose inconspicuously of their weapons on the way.

It is often so easy to identify the wrong in others, and condemn their sins as we quote chapter and verse. But as we come under the searching gaze of a Holy God we can maybe begin to loosen our grip on the stones we were about to hurl, and wince as they strike **us** on the foot. All our arguments melt away; we note how impossible it is to remove the splinter from the eye of our brothers and sisters while our thinking is so unbalanced, due to the log in our own.

When Jesus looked up the only person in the Temple court was the poor shivering girl. Where were the crowds who had risen early to hear him? Had his followers also searched their hearts, hung their heads and crept away?

We know the answer to the question '*Has no-one condemned you?*' There is no record of the girl's confession so no reason to expect forgiveness from Jesus. When the Son of God says, '*neither do I condemn you*', we can learn from his compassion, empathy and love. His instruction, '*Go, and sin no more*' (Authorised Version), is a challenge to us all, for all have sinned and come short of the standard raised before us by God.

> How differently we can view the sins of others when we see them through the murky waters of our own past.

It matters that we care

Mary Hopper writes about the importance of true care and compassion

BIBLE REF:
Mark 5: 22 - 34
Luke 4: 1 - 48

BIBLE VERSE:
Daughter, your faith has healed you. Go in peace and be freed from your suffering.

We should remind ourselves that this woman should never have been at the centre of this event; well, that was according to the law. Her disability meant she was a socially unclean outcast - unable to go to church or have fellowship with friends and family.

She was no doubt feeling guilty for being there - embarrassed and afraid that others would find out what was wrong with her - but she was desperate. No doctor had been able to help her and now she was extremely poor - financially, physically and emotionally drained.

The news of the healing touch of Jesus was spreading, so the woman decided to try him, perhaps as a last desperate measure. There were crowds of people and in her physically compromised state she could not get close to him; but she was not deterred. She only wanted to touch his clothing; she did not want any fuss and wanted to remain unnoticed. She pressed through and was amazed that the minute she touched his robes he stopped and turned towards her. She was also aware that her twelve-year-old debilitating illness had completely left her.

She may have been frightened of the reaction of both Jesus and the crowd as they came to realise the unacceptable, unclean company they had been keeping. But when she testified before him and the crowd, he gently turned to her and addressed her as 'Daughter' - the closest of relationships she could have with him. He assured her that her healing was the result of her faith and dismissed her with his peace - what a gift - the sense of peace that passes human understanding: that sense of belonging and being of worth and value.

Jesus was busy, but not too busy to acknowledge her. Jesus had time to listen - he affirmed her. Jesus valued her so much he did not just want her to be healed, he wanted to speak with her. What a huge impact that must have had on her - someone who felt so unclean and such a worthless outcast - in dialogue with the Messiah!

God may well test our faith; he may ask us to give our testimony. But we can be assured he has our best interests at heart, and that means not only dealing with physical symptoms, but with the emotional and spiritual ones too. This is not just for us, but for those to whom we minister in his name - can those of us involved in healthcare of any sort learn from Jesus here?

Caring matters. It matters for the one for whom we care. It matters to us. Above all it matters to our Saviour - the Lord Jesus Christ.

Can those of us involved in healthcare of any sort learn from Jesus here?

The Gospel goes global

Steve Fouch challenges us to step out of our cultural prejudices and comfort zones

BIBLE REF:
Acts 10

BIBLE VERSE:
...and he said to them, 'You yourselves know that it is unlawful for a Jew to associate with or to visit a Gentile; but God has shown me that I should not call anyone profane or unclean'.
(New Revised Standard Version)

This story is a turning point for the church. Until now, the Apostles understood Jesus' teaching as being for the Jews. There had been the odd example of outsiders being welcomed into the Church - eg the Ethiopian eunuch in Acts 8: 25 - 40, but now God does something radical. Not only does he call Peter to go to a Gentile household, he actually sends an angel to the Gentile first.

When Peter makes this statement in verse 28, it is easy to gloss over just how radical a statement he is making. For a Jew, to enter a Gentile home made one unclean - requiring daylong purification rituals before going back into normal Jewish society. Furthermore, this was not any old Gentile; it was a serving, senior officer in the hated army of Roman occupation. This story is often shown from the perspective of Cornelius' conversion, but the reality is that Peter underwent as radical a conversion as Cornelius. For he at last grasped the great truth Jesus had been trying to teach him - the Gospel was for **all** peoples, regardless of culture, social status or background. And he had to get over his prejudices towards the Romans, and Roman soldiers in particular pretty quickly. Imagine a Hamas militant and an Israeli settler sitting down together and accepting one another in the same way. That's how radical a conversion Peter had to undergo.

Jesus had clearly demonstrated several times during his ministry that the Gospel was for everyone (think of the Syro-Phoenician woman in Matthew 15: 21 - 28, or the Samaritan woman in John 4 or the Roman centurion in Matthew 8: 5 - 13). This must have been very offensive to the Jews around Jesus.

But are we any different? Do we think our own brand of Christianity or our own cultural expression is God's chosen one? Are we in danger of missing out? And do we look on other types of Christians with contempt because they do things differently to us? Paul had to deal with this a lot during his ministry, and even had to have a go at Peter (who by now should have known better!) for having double standards in dealing with Christians of another culture (Galatians 2: 11 - 14).

The big shock about worshipping with Christians from other corners of the globe can be to find how different Christians can be culturally and still worship the same God, and how much of what we take as Gospel is in fact cultural. We need Christians of every culture and colour, because the picture of the Kingdom in Isaiah and Revelation shows us that the final ingathering will be from all corners of the Earth - and there will be no uniformity in heaven - praise God!

The final ingathering will be from all corners of the Earth - and there will be no uniformity in heaven - praise God!

ACTION
Get involved with a local church rather than staying with the Western expatriate church. Find out how others worship, learn from their ways of following Jesus, however alien they may seem at first. You may have more to learn and receive than to give, but don't be afraid to share what God has given you as well.

FURTHER READING
Galatians 3: 26 - 29
Isaiah 2: 1 - 4; 66: 20 - 22
Revelation 7: 9 - 10

Jesus withdrew

Mary Hopper writes about persistence and perseverance

BIBLE REF:
Matthew 15: 21 - 28
Mark 7: 24 - 30

BIBLE VERSE:
Jesus left that place and went to the vicinity of Tyre. He entered a house and did not want anyone to know it; yet he could not keep his presence secret.

After the death of his friend, John the Baptist, Jesus went off with his disciples to a quiet spot near Bethsaida (Luke 9: 10), apparently for a time of reflection. However, things did not quite go as planned, and soon the shore of the Sea of Galilee was buzzing with the crowds that followed him.

In similar circumstances we might become upset and consider it was unfair - this was 'private time'. But Jesus had compassion on the people, and began to heal the sick and infirm. There was no way he could turn them away. Then much to the amazement of his disciples he fed them - all 5,000 men, plus their families!

Then he went up into the hills alone, to spend time with his Father. Later he crossed the lake (!) to help his disciples, who were in trouble on the water. When they reached the shore, people hurried to bring their sick friends for him to heal. With no rest or sleep for Jesus, the round of healing and preaching and teaching began again.

Shortly after this they set off to Tyre and Sidon. Here Jesus had the encounter with the Greek woman who begged him to go and drive away a demon from her daughter. So what was the reaction of the desperately worn out, wanting a rest, end of his tether, sleepless Saviour? He did not immediately say anything. The disciples wanted to get rid of her. Jesus apparently was not going to do anything. This woman must have felt desperate. What was happening with her daughter right now? Was she being thrown around, was she convulsing? What danger was she in?

The men who were with Jesus spoke over her head - as if she was not there - telling him to send her away. She must have felt humiliated to be basically ignored. Then, anger, rejection and disappointment, when the only words that Jesus did say to her appeared highly insulting. It would have been easy to curse him and walk away having lost her faith. She didn't even argue her claim on him was as good as that of any Jew. She didn't plead for her rights at all. Rather she threw herself at his feet and cried for help, casting herself on his mercy.

This woman showed great insight, patience, perseverance and humility. Her focus was on her daughter's needs and not on her own rights, and she was even prepared to be seen as a dog under the table if it meant that her loved one could receive some of the Master's crumbs of grace.

The Bible never promises to answer our prayers immediately, and the Lord does at times test our faith for our eventual good.

We can be assured that:

- God is faithful, and will not allow us to be tempted beyond what we can bear. But when we are tempted he will provide a way out - so that we can stand up under that temptation. (1 Corinthians 10: 13)
- When we suffer trials and grief, they have come that our faith may be refined and we may be proved genuine (1 Peter 1: 6, 7). Faith is tested when it is taken to the limits of our endurance - something that only God knows and can determine.

> The Bible never promises to answer our prayers immediately.

PRAYER & ACTION
When it feels like it just is not fair, let us say like this woman, 'Yes Lord, I believe You know what is best for me - I am a sinner. I deserve none of Your blessings, but I throw myself before You trusting myself to Your grace and mercy.'

Here is a trustworthy saying
that deserves full acceptance:
Christ Jesus came into
the world to save sinners.

1 Timothy 1:15

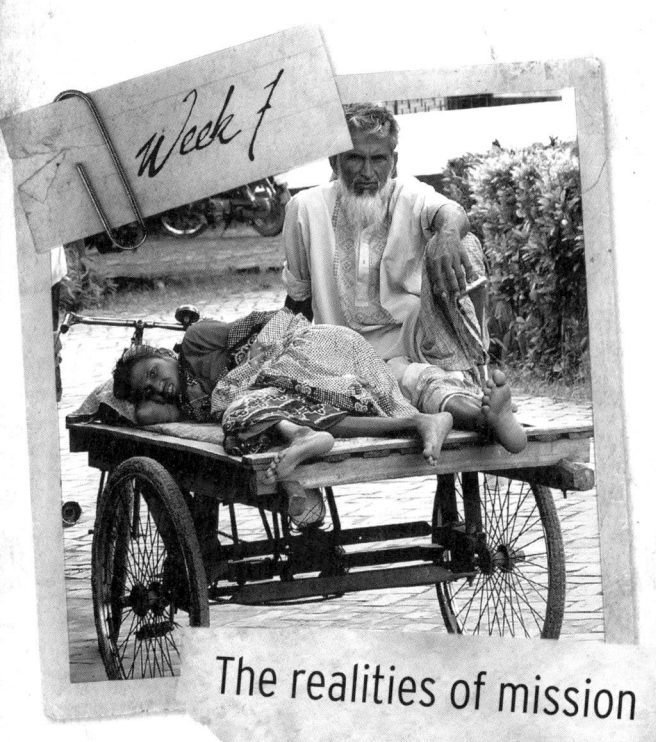

Week 7

The realities of mission

Just little me

Kate Cheesman writes about relying on God rather than ourselves

BIBLE REF:
1 Corinthians 1: 27 - 29

BIBLE VERSE:
God chose the foolish things of the world to shame the wise; God chose the weak things of the world to shame the strong.

It took me a long time to get round to writing anything for this book. It was partly because I was busy and partly because I didn't know what to write. I'm not an amazing Christian with wise things to say and I felt a bit inadequate.

I was praying about what on earth I could say when I realised that I had been right: I am not an amazing Christian and I am inadequate. I am so grateful that God asks me to do anything for him when he knows even better than I do that I'm not the best person to ask. He hasn't asked me to serve him because he needed me and knew I'd be good at it, but just because he wanted to ask me.

I had a fantastic medical elective in Brazil. Everything worked out so well, not because of anything I had planned but because God blessed me lots and fitted everything together so perfectly. I had been worried before I went that maybe I wouldn't be able to do anything much, especially as my Portuguese isn't very good. While I was there I was invited to more hospitals and clinics than I could fit into the time I had. I managed to use enough Portuguese, and I had the privilege of caring for an abandoned baby for a month.

These verses in Corinthians reminded me that no Christian is especially good on their own but just because of what God does. God asks us to use what he has given us and that is always enough. Nobody can say that they don't have enough or they aren't good enough to do anything for God yet. If anything, that makes them even better qualified to be used by God. He likes to choose the foolish, the weak, the lowly and the despised.

He hasn't asked me to serve him because he needed me and knew I'd be good at it, but just because he wanted to ask me.

FURTHER READING
1 Samuel 16: 1 - 13
Luke 21: 1 - 4
Matthew 25: 14 - 30

Mission: top priority

Mark Marno writes about the importance of sharing the Good News about Jesus

BIBLE REF:
Romans 1: 16 - 17

BIBLE VERSE:
I am not ashamed of the gospel, because it is the power of God for the salvation of everyone who believes: first for the Jew, then for the Gentile.

In the rush of everyday life it can be so easy to get our priorities wrong. One of the biggest criticisms of my work as a newly qualified staff nurse is my poor prioritisation skills. I get into work fresh and ready to take on a new day with new challenges. I'm psyched. Ready and raring to go. I know what nursing care I have to give, what other tasks I've got to do and when. I have time set aside to do all of these things but somewhere along the line, usually quite early on in my case, it all goes to pot. I get distracted by less urgent or important things, often because of good intentions, and an inability to say 'no' when asked to help others. The fact is I've lost sight of what I started out focused on.

Similarly, it can be easy to lose focus of the objectives in mission. The input of healthcare providers, especially in less developed countries, is much needed and it is right that some Christians should feel a desire to serve people in this way (both at home and abroad). What distinguishes the Christian healthcare provider from the non-Christian, however, is our ability also to give people something far greater than healthcare; an opportunity to hear the gospel.

The main point of mission is to share the gospel (**good news** - what an understatement!) with people. Paul tells us why this is far greater than mere healthcare, *'it is the power of God for the salvation of everyone who believes'* (v16). When we read on in Romans, and put into context what this salvation is **from** and how the only way to obtain it is through Jesus, it is difficult not to recognise its significance to everyone. The gospel is not something to be ashamed of but rather something glorious and essential to share with others, if we truly desire to help them and see them saved.

As Christian healthcare providers we must remember that we are Christians first, and as Christians our top priority is God and seeing him glorified. We should be wanting to tell everyone of his greatness and what he has done for us. True we are not preachers, we are healthcare providers but we are healthcare providers second to being Christians. Our work as healthcare providers, whether overseas or at home, should be viewed in the context of glorifying God with our words and actions.

> The gospel is not something to be ashamed of but rather something glorious and essential to share with others.

FURTHER READING
Romans 1: 18 - 3: 28
Mark 10

Mission:
right here, right now!

Mark Marno writes about being witnesses to Jesus where we live and work

BIBLE REF:
Colossians 4: 2 - 6

BIBLE VERSE:
And pray for us, too, that God may open a door for our message, so that we may proclaim the mystery of Christ, for which I am in chains.

The Bible makes absolutely clear that we, as Christians, should be firmly focused on Christ, longing to see him glorified in all that we do, and working with joy convinced of our future eternity with him (read Colossians 3: 1 - 3, 17, 23 - 24).

As a kid in Northern Ireland I dreamed of journeying to some far-flung land to meet some unknown people who were in need of Christ and with whom I could share the gospel. Now here I am trying to do this, in London. Hopefully the fact that there are lots of people around you in Uni and in hospitals who are in need of Christ, both patients and colleagues, has not escaped your attention. This is your mission field! That is not to say that some day God won't call you to serve him elsewhere but it is a reminder that he does call you right here and right now to serve him.

Before getting carried away with the romanticism many associate with missionary work, it is worthwhile considering just how you are getting involved in 'missionary' work where you live right now.

Are you praying?
Our experience of life should convince us that our solo efforts in running our own lives are agonisingly inadequate. We need to be praying with respect to every area of our lives, not least our evangelism. It can be so easy to lose sight of the big picture - the state of unrighteousness that the world is in and where it is heading without God (as we saw in yesterday's reading: Romans 1: 16 - 3: 28).

- Have you got a passion to see people you know saved? Are you praying for them?
- Are you praying for wisdom and strength in sharing the gospel with them?
- Do you pray for others in the world to share the gospel with people who need Christ?

Do you make the most of every opportunity?
Relationships play an immense role in sharing the gospel. If people notice a difference in the way you relate to them and live your life - with God as top priority - they are more likely to seek out the reason behind this. When this happens it is best to be prepared. Someone once said that the best type of spontaneity is planned spontaneity!

Are you wise in the way that you act towards others? Do you have an intentional relationship with people (one that is thought out, and considers how best you can serve both them and God in making him known)?

Do you know what you would say if someone asked why you have different priorities or why you have the hope that you have (1 Peter 3: 15)? Do you know the gospel well enough yourself to be confident in doing this?

Are You a Missionary Right here, Right Now?

> Relationships play an immense role in sharing the gospel.

Dare to be different

Mark Marno writes about finding the courage to stand up for what is right

BIBLE REF:
Daniel 6

BIBLE VERSE:
Three times a day he got down on his knees and prayed, giving thanks to his God, just as he had done before.

On the team's journey to the isolated little village where we would be working in Ghana, we stopped to stock up on supplies in the nearest big city. As we drove away from a supermarket several members of the team witnessed an incident in which a teenage boy was knocked to the floor by some older boys who threatened to kick him. Previous to this the boy had been acting peculiarly, brandishing a stick at some younger boys around him, and had given us the impression that he may have been mentally ill. Nobody on the team intervened to find out the full story or to help the boy. When later discussed by the team it seemed that what had stopped us from intervening had not been a sense that the boy had brought it on himself or a fear for our own safety in the situation. Rather it was an acceptance that we were in a different culture, where things that may be unacceptable in the UK may be perfectly normal, that seemed to be the overriding reason why we didn't intervene.

Although it is certainly wise and advisable to become acquainted with differences in culture when working abroad, we as Christians must also recognise the Christian culture inside us in the way that we interact with others. It can be extremely difficult to stand up and be counted for doing what is right when it goes against the culture that you find yourself in. Of course this can be equally true of the home environment at university, in the hospital or at home with family, as it can be in some far-flung country.

The way in which we relate to or interact with people cannot be determined by what people around us are doing but rather it must be determined by looking at what God would have us do.

During my time in Ghana one big question came up in a few difficult situations - what would Jesus do? The WWJD craze has, of course, become very popular amongst young Christians today. We have wristbands, badges and who knows what else displayed on people, in an attempt to remind them to consider how to live their lives in a way honouring to God. Unfortunately, however, all too often little attention is paid to such reminders once the novelty has worn off (I speak from experience).

If we are serious as Christians about wanting to honour God in our actions, then we need to start with God and seeking his desire. Much more than simply asking ourselves 'What would Jesus do?', we need to study Jesus' life as found in the Bible and view him as a role model - the perfect example of how to live our lives as a living sacrifice to God. God has revealed himself to us both in Christ and in his word, the Bible. What an awesome privilege this is. In studying the Bible we receive guidance on how to live our lives and we must not allow popular culture to supercede this, whether that be in the UK or anywhere else in God's world.

> It can be extremely difficult to stand up and be counted for doing what is right when it goes against the culture that you find yourself in.

FURTHER READING
Luke 10: 25 - 37
Daniel 1
Romans 6

Loneliness

Mark Marno writes about dealing with loneliness

BIBLE REF:
John 12: 32

BIBLE VERSE:
But a time is coming, and has come, when you will be scattered, each to his own home. You will leave me all alone. Yet I am not alone, for My Father is with me.

Anti-malarials can be fun! I had some fantastically colourful and slightly scary dreams under the influence of Lariam whilst in Ghana. I didn't need Lariam, however, to fuel many of my other reactions. Loneliness hit hard when I left my teammates to spend my second month in Ghana working at the opposite end of the country with locals whom I had never met. Having been in the very close company of the team for three and a half weeks, I was suddenly left to discover a completely new and very different part of the country by myself. For a considerable amount of time on the bus journey to the South and then settling into my new accommodation, I had not spoken to anybody that I knew. I was feeling very lonely. At night I dreamt of family and friends back home and of the teammates I had left behind. During the day I had plenty of spare time to think about what the others in the team were doing in our normal everyday routine.

Perhaps you can relate to this experience of loneliness. Perhaps the exciting novelty stage of your time overseas has worn off and you long to be surrounded by people whom you know and who know you. Perhaps the thought hadn't even crossed your mind until now - sorry for bringing it up in that case!

It was a great help for me at that time to be reminded of the fact that Jesus knew what it was like to be in a similar, only much more serious, situation. Betrayed and abandoned by his friends, having known all along that this would happen, Jesus was taken, beaten, falsely accused, put on trial, rejected and despised by his own people, who demanded his crucifixion. As you picture Christ walking to Calvary, it is hard to imagine a more lonely scene. The King of kings, by rights the Ruler of everyone past, present and future, was rejected by everyone, even his closest having abandoned him.

Yet despite the loneliness of the situation, Christ knew that he was not alone. Jesus knew that he and the Father are One and that the Father was with him at that time. In the same way we as Christians, united to Christ, can be confident of God's presence with us. God has given us his Holy Spirit as he promised he would (John 16: 5 - 16), he has promised that he will never leave us (Hebrews 13: 5) and he has told us that nothing can separate us, his children, from his love (Romans 8: 35 - 39).

To be reminded that the greatest friend that it is possible to have is still around and loving you is a sure-fire way to fight the feelings of loneliness. All too often the manic pace of life on the wards can distract you from giving quality time to the development of such a relationship. Make the most of the time that you have now to develop your relationship with God. Pray to him. Read his word. Grow in your knowledge of and faith in God.

> The greatest friend that it is possible to have is still around and loving you.

FURTHER READING
Mark 10: 32 - 34
John 16: 25 - 33

God's sovereignty: who's in control?

Mark Marno reminds us that God is in control in every situation

BIBLE REF:
Matthew 8: 23 - 27

BIBLE VERSE:
What kind of man is this? Even the winds and the waves obey him!

Journals are hard work. They require enthusiasm, discipline and reflection - all of which are very hard work for me! The first entry in my journal of my time in Ghana is proof of this. The date is Friday 21st July 2000 and the first words written are these:

OK, so I've cheated. I haven't actually bought this journal yet. I won't buy it for another 2 days. In fact it gets worse. The day I'm starting this is Tuesday 15th August ...

As the first few days of my journal confirm, a big issue for me before leaving for Ghana was one of fear. Maybe not fear of physical danger (although the experience of driving into London for the first time did seem to pose a real threat to my life!) but rather fears that the team chosen to go to Ghana for one month with Tearfund may not bond when we first meet, and that there may be tension and problems throughout the trip. A fear that the twelve of us couldn't do this on our own. These fears were shared by others, and as a team and as individuals we brought them to God in prayer, recognising again and again with every new situation that he was in control.

It's great to read through my journal now and again, and recognise the fact that God truly was in control in situations I had been concerned about because they were out of my control. Comparing my concerns about finances, travel, safety, illness, team dynamics and the timing of events with just how these potential problems panned out under God's control, and how he used these circumstances to teach me and help me grow in my faith really does humble me. Why did I ever have any fear about what would happen when I knew that God was in control?

Consider who God is. He is GOD - omnipotent, creator of all things, sovereign, Lord of all, and ruler over everything he has made. Trust him!

> God truly was in control in situations I had been concerned about because they were out of my control.

FURTHER READING
Proverbs 3: 5 - 8
Judges 7
1 Samuel 17

Week 1
Day 4 # Walking with God

Steve Fouch writes about walking with God in every moment

BIBLE REF:
Micah 6: 8

BIBLE VERSE:
He has told you, O mortal, what is good; and what does the LORD require of you but to do justice, and to love kindness, and to walk humbly with your God?

(New Revised Standard Version)

It is easy to get caught up in work, in the doing of things for God, in pursuing our careers, or even just getting to the end of a shift with physical and mental health relatively intact. Sometimes everything seems to revolve around our work, our social life, our reading - it all crowds in.

There is a saying that *'the good is the enemy of the best'* - and that goes double for serving God. What motivated you to go overseas for your elective? Was it to get an exciting experience, to try something different? Was it to see and learn something new of God, or was it a desire to serve him? All these are good reasons - and I would be the last to decry them, but they can be the enemy of *the best*.

But what is the best, you ask? Micah sums it up. Yes, show the fruit of the Spirit in justice and kindness, these are essential parts of our daily walk (see Amos 5: 24, Jeremiah 7: 3 - 6), but they are not *the walk*. *The walk* is with God - it is in journeying with him through each and every moment of each and every day that we find *the best* and not just *the good*.

Hosea 6: 6 and Zephaniah 2: 3 speak more of this - God wants our presence, our focus to be on him, not on his gifts, not on his work, but on him. All else then flows from that.

Each day is a journey, part of a longer 'journey of our lives', as Dante describes it in *The Divine Comedy*. We may have many different companions on that journey, coming and going at different times, some staying for longer than others, some walking more closely with us than others, but there is only One who walks with us all day, every day, for the whole of our lives. And it is his company above all other things that we should cultivate.

The walk is with God – it is in journeying with him through each and every moment of each and every day.

FURTHER READING
Mark 12: 29 -31
Psalm 71: 17 - 18

Those who hope in the Lord
will renew their strength.
They will soar on wings
like eagles; they will run
and not grow weary, they
will walk and not be faint.

Isaiah 40:31

Rising above
the day-to-day

Finding rest

Peggy Burton writes about resting in God in the midst of the busyness of work

BIBLE REF:
Matthew 11: 28

BIBLE VERSE:
Come unto Me all you who are weary and burdened and I will give you rest.

The world today is full of hustle and bustle. Everyone seems to be in a hurry, and everything needs to be done now. This seems doubly to be the case in a busy hospital with too few staff and too many patients! In such an environment, how can anyone be still and find rest?

In Genesis 2: 2 - 3 we see how God had finished the work he was doing by the Seventh Day of Creation, so he took that day to rest, and so made it a rest day for humanity as well (Exodus 20: 11; 34: 21). This is more than an opportunity for rest, it is a command, and even more it is a gift of God, for we rest not just from our own labours, but in the Holy Spirit we find a true 'Sabbath' rest in the presence of God himself (Isaiah 63: 14; Hebrews 4: 9 - 11). It is something we have to take a hold of, not something that just happens. Rest is something that God want us to take up, and it is our burdens he asks us to lay down at the foot of his cross (Matthew 11: 30).

It is so easy to put off taking a break, spending time with God, or just resting with friends when the pressure is on. But this is not slacking or wasting time, it is a divine command, something God has created us for, and something that he offers us if we will but come to him. Work can become a burden of slavery, even when it is done in his name, so don't let it, because he came to free us from all yokes of burden (Galatians 5:1).

So let God give you rest.

PRAYER & ACTION

- Carve out time for him. Make a decision to take that Sabbath rest day once in every seven, and in every day find that time of rest to receive what God wants to give you.

It is so easy to put off taking a break, spending time with God, or just resting with friends when the pressure is on.

Strength for the weary

Steve Fouch looks at how we can find God's strength when we've run out

BIBLE REF:
Isaiah 40: 29 - 31

BIBLE VERSE:
He gives power to the faint, and strengthens the powerless. Even youths will faint and be weary, and the young will fall exhausted, but those who wait for the LORD shall renew their strength, they shall mount up with wings like eagles, they shall run and not be weary, they shall walk and not faint.

Have you ever got to the end of a week, or even a shift, and felt you had nothing left to give? Then suddenly something crops up, an emergency as you are about to leave the ward, or a friend in need on the phone when you get home? You feel inside of you, 'I have nothing left to give', yet somehow you do, not knowing where the strength comes from.

I have small children, and after a long day at work, feeling all I want to do is curl up with a book or in front of the telly and rest, my children instead demand attention, play, and someone to share their day's triumphs and disasters with. I somehow have the strength, even at the end of myself to do this, and take joy in it.

Maybe sometimes we don't find we have that extra bit of strength, because there really is nothing else left to give, and afterwards we feel ashamed because there was more that we should have done for that patient or friend. But we are, after all, only human.

God offers us something remarkable. When we get to the end of ourselves, we find he is there waiting for us with Eagle's wings to lift us. Paul exulted in this miracle of grace when he wrote 'he [Jesus] said to me, "My grace is sufficient for you, for My power is made perfect in weakness." Therefore I will boast all the more gladly about my weaknesses, so that Christ's power may rest on me' (2 Corinthians 12: 9).

So, when you come to the end of your human resources, as so often we all do, do not despair. Because that is when, if we call upon him, God meets us with a supply of something greater than our human strength, something more powerful and miraculous than all we can accomplish by our effort. Then we too can rejoice like Paul in our weakness, because through it, God's strength is seen.

Sometimes we don't find we have that extra bit of strength, because there really is nothing else left to give.

FURTHER READING
2 Corinthians 11: 29; 12: 5
Genesis 49: 24 - 25
Philippians 4: 13

The Martha syndrome

Helen Malcolm underlines the importance of taking time to be with God

BIBLE REF:
Luke 10: 41 - 42

BIBLE VERSE:
'Martha, Martha,' the Lord answered, 'you are worried and upset about many things, but only one thing is needed.'

The Martha syndrome is not described in any textbook and yet it is easily recognisable in our patients, our families and friends, and in ourselves. It has two diagnostic features - the need to be continually busy, and anxiety about getting everything done.

In the story of Martha and Mary we are reminded to get our priorities right. Jesus gently corrected Martha for her anxious concern over the practical, physical things of life, whereas Mary was content to sit at Jesus' feet and listen to what he was saying. Jesus himself took time out from the demands of his ministry, to draw aside to be with God and to encourage his disciples to do the same. We need to ensure that we make time to just 'be', to sit with God and hear what he has to say to us, to hear things we cannot hear if we are always 'doing'.

To be properly able to care for our patients, we need to care for ourselves. To show patience, reassurance, hope and confidence, and to equip our patients with the skills to go on with life - even in the face of illness and despair - we must ourselves be calm, unrushed, and attentive. We need to be able to emphasise by our lives the important features of health and wholeness - we need to show that we can relate to the Creator through Christ, even when the physical body is suffering.

PRAYER

God of peace, You taught that in returning and in rest we shall be saved, in quietness and in confidence shall be our strength: by the power of Your Spirit lift us to Your presence, where we may be still and know that You are God.

May the peace of God my Father
Rule my life in everything,
That I may be calm to comfort
Sick and sorrowing.

Kate Barclay Wilkinson (d. 1928)

We need to ensure that we make time to just 'be', to sit with God.

FURTHER READING
Luke 10: 36 - 42
John 14: 25 - 27

Heartcry for mission

A challenge from Sophia Lamb to find
God's heart for the lost

BIBLE REF:
Mark 16: 15

BIBLE VERSE:
Go into all the
world and
preach the
good news to
all creation.

Apartments shook and collapsed. Over 2,000 died in the earthquake that left parts of central Taiwan devastated. I watched on television and wondered about my friends, the young missionary couple with their new baby, and the girl I went to China with. At least eternity held no fear for them, but what of the others? Having lived without Christ, must they face eternity without him too? Could I have been more directly involved in Mission? Could I have introduced some of these people to Jesus?

Like others, I have reasons for not being more involved. I am an untrained, unpaid medical student with a full and busy life. But are these valid reasons, or are they inadequate excuses that I put up to prevent me from being involved in Mission now?

Although I cannot move overseas, I can reach out locally and further afield during holidays and electives. Letters and emails open the whole world to me. Again, is my 'poor student' status a sufficient excuse for not giving? European countries spend billions each year on luxuries! It has been said that living and spending mindless of the poor is being mindless of God. Perhaps a more simple life would enable me to give more towards mission? Finally, though busy, I could pray more. *'The harvest is plentiful but the workers are few. Ask the Lord of the harvest, therefore, to send out workers into his harvest field.'* (Matthew 9: 37 - 38)

God's heart is for mission - to reach everyone in every part of his world. No matter how confined or poor or busy, we can find means of being part of mission. God has a role for each one of us that stretches beyond home, classroom and hospital walls. There are excuses and obstacles, but the Bible tells us to go! Let us do something about it today.

> God has a role for each one of us that stretches beyond home, classroom and hospital walls.

FURTHER READING
Acts 1: 8
Matthew 28: 18 - 20

We don't know what to do!

Ian Spillman writes about focusing on God, and not our problems

BIBLE REF:
2 Chronicles 20: 12

BIBLE VERSE:
...we have no power to face this vast army that is attacking us.

The story behind this verse is of a small nation, faced by overwhelming odds, and experiencing the frustration and fear also felt by so many today. Even in professional life, we face vast problems. Yet we have a choice as to how we react: do we panic, or pray? Prayer helps us to find proper perspective.

God's power is great. He has proved himself sovereign and faithful in the past and the same is true of him now as it was then (Hebrews 13: 8). He is completely trustworthy and we can rely on his promises. *'Do not be afraid or discouraged because of this vast army. For the battle is not yours, but God's'* (2 Chronicles 20: 15). At times of crisis we are not to run anywhere but to him (2 Chronicles 6: 15 - 17). If the crisis is of our own making, we need to turn in repentance (6: 24 - 25) but then can rely on his mercy. The focus is not to be so much on the problem itself as on God's ability to resolve it.

We gradually learn to understand that following God's direction and leading does not mean leading a problem-free life. It can be the opposite. Yet through his death and resurrection, our Lord Jesus invites us to share in his victory (1 John 5: 5). We may also share some of his suffering, in a world so much at odds with him (Philippians 3: 10).

Recognising our own inadequacy demands humility, best found in reflection on his great might and everlasting love.

*We go in faith, our own great
weakness feeling,
    And needing more each day
Thy grace to know:
    Yet from our hearts a song
of triumph pealing,
    We rest on Thee and in Thy name we go.*
                    Edith Gilling Cherry (d. 1897)

Following God's direction and leading does not mean leading a problem-free life. It can be the opposite.

FURTHER READING
2 Chronicles 20: 1 - 17

Sorting out priorities

Ernst Jacobson asks 'is the work of building God's church a priority for us?'

BIBLE REF:
Haggai 1: 5

BIBLE VERSE:
Now this is what the LORD Almighty says: 'Give careful thought to your ways'.

After the exiles' return to Israel from Babylon, Ezra and Haggai tell us how they eventually started to rebuild the temple. They then came under attack from the heathen people around them, and gave up the work (Ezra 4: 24). Do we, too, lose courage when we meet resistance? The Israelites excused themselves by saying that the time had not yet come to rebuild the house of the Lord (Haggai 1: 2).

However, the word of the Lord came to them through Haggai: '*Is it a time for you yourselves to be living in your panelled houses, while this house remains a ruin? ... Give careful thought to your ways.*' He went on to point out that they were still short of food and drink, clothing and cash - all a direct result of their unfaithfulness. (Haggai 1: 3 - 6, 9)

Does the Lord blame people for living in nicely built and well-furnished houses? I don't think so. He is saying, 'If you can afford to live in such houses, you can afford to build my house'. In its widest sense, the Lord's house today is his church. We should make a priority of support for missionary and evangelistic work, which spread the gospel and help the poor.

If you can afford to live in such houses, you can afford to build my house.

Is this how I spend my time, my education and skill, my money? Is there a disproportion between what I spend on myself and the 'temple'? Do I spend all my time making money and neglect my family, or fail to enjoy the fellowship of other Christians in the local church? When the Israelites obeyed the voice of the Lord their God, his Spirit remained with them and they were blessed (Haggai 2: 5). May we have the same experience as we sort out our priorities.

FURTHER READING
Ezra 5: 1 - 5; 7: 27 - 28
Matthew 6: 25 - 34

We're on a road to somewhere, come on inside

Steve Fouch writes about mission

BIBLE REF:
Revelation 21: 1 - 8

BIBLE VERSE:

Then I heard a loud voice call from the throne, 'You see this City? Here God lives among men. He will make his home among them; they shall be his people, and he will be their God.'

(The Jerusalem Bible)

Where are you going? Hopefully, by this stage in your elective the answer is either 'on holiday' or 'back home'. It's a question we ask every day - am I going to theatre or to the wards, on the rounds or to a teaching session? Am I off out with my friends after work or going home to swot up with only a microwave dinner and *EastEnders* for company? Maybe you ask the questions, 'Where will I be in a year, two years, five years, ten years? Where is my career going?'

In the secular world, the questions don't usually get much further than this. The title for this section comes from an old *Talking heads* song 'We're on a Road to Nowhere'. That's the reality most people are too scared to contemplate, that we're heading towards oblivion. Because after all, however much we try to cover it up, death awaits us all (barring the Lord's return). So no wonder the long-term question doesn't get asked - it is just too difficult to face.

But as Christians we know that we **are** going somewhere. Home, where we belong (Philippians 3: 20), to be with God. To a world of peace, healing, joy and hope (v4 of our text). This world is a world in which we are strangers, simply passing through. It is a transient place that will eventually pass away to be replaced by the New Creation to which we now belong (vs1 - 2, and 2 Corinthians 5: 17).

Everything is transformed by this simple fact. What matters to us? Passing that exam, getting that pay rise, moving into that nice house, getting a satellite dish? Or is it that when we face the judgment, we can do so in confidence? What matters - what we have here and now, or our new life in Christ that starts now but becomes complete in Eternity? (Philippians 3: 7 - 9). Suddenly, all our current trials and tribulations seem like nothing. In Tony Campolo's words, *'It's Friday, but Sunday's coming!'*

But it's not just enough to kick back and coast home (2 Peter 3: 10 - 14). Far from it - the awful reality of the judgment that is coming (Revelation 20: 11 - 15) should spur us on to see the gospel shared with the lost, the broken-hearted comforted, the blind receive sight, the sick healed (Isaiah 61: 1 - 3). Do we want to stand before our Lord on Judgment Day and realise that the World has been lost because we never told anyone?

Mission is about just that - wherever we are, whatever we do, helping people to discover the truth and showing the love of God in action. We are working with a purpose because we know that we are on the Road to Somewhere, that all this world offers us is trivia, complete dross compared to what is coming. We're on our way to the New Jerusalem; I don't know about you, but I want to be bringing a lot of people along with me when I get inside **that** City!

Mission is about just this - wherever we are, whatever we do, helping people to discover the truth and showing the love of God in action.

ACTION
Ask yourself this question: if you knew that the Lord was coming back tomorrow, what would your priorities be? What would matter to you most? Then pray that God would help you get your priorities sorted out in line with his will, and ask him to help you live your life so it will count into Eternity.

FURTHER READING
Isaiah 65: 17 - 25
1 Corinthians 15: 50 - 58

Resources

Online resources for healthcare & medical mission

- **Mission Resources Directory**
  Online resource directory of useful contacts, web links
  and information for those interested or involved
  in healthcare & medical mission.

- **Student Elective Handbooks**
  Help and resources for medical, nursing,
  dental and therapy students planning electives

- **Elective Directories**
  Contact details of organisations and hospitals
  who take elective students

These publications and more are available to download
at **www.cmf.org.uk/internationalministries**

Contact us
CMF International Department
6 Marshalsea Road
London SE1 1HL
Tel: 020 7234 9669
Email: healthserve@cmf.org.uk

Other publications from CMF

Preparing for your Medical Elective
A handbook to help you plan
and prepare

Working Abroad
A handbook for those investigating
possibilities of working abroad

I could do that!
15 stories of people who've worked in
different settings around the world

CMF produces a wide range of publications
which can be ordered from **www.cmf.org.uk**

Notes